Table of Contents

Preface

In January 2018 I started the preparation of a programming course targeting students without programming experience. I wanted to use Julia, but I found that there existed no book with the purpose of learning to program with Julia as the first programming language. There are wonderful tutorials that explain Julia's key concepts, but none of them pay sufficient attention to learning how to think like a programmer.

I knew the book *Think Python* by Allen Downey, which contains all the key ingredients to learn to program properly. However, this book was based on the Python programming language. My first draft of the course notes was a melting pot of all kinds of reference works, but the longer I worked on it, the more the content started to resemble the chapters of *Think Python*. Soon, the idea of developing my course notes as a port of that book to Julia came to fruition.

All the material was available as Jupyter notebooks in a GitHub repository. After I posted a message on the Julia Discourse site about the progress of my course, the feedback was overwhelming. A book about basic programming concepts with Julia as the first programming language was apparently a missing link in the Julia universe. I contacted Allen to ask if I could start an official port of *Think Python* to Julia, and his answer was immediate: "Go for it!" He put me in touch with his editor at O'Reilly Media, and a year later I was putting the finishing touches on this book.

It was a bumpy ride. In August 2018 Julia v1.0 was released, and like all my fellow Julia programmers I had to do a migration of the code. All the examples in the book were tested during the conversion of the source files to O'Reilly-compatible AsciiDoc files. Both the toolchain and the example code had to be made Julia v1.0–compliant. Luckily, there are no lectures to give in August....

I hope you enjoy working with this book, and that it helps you learn to program and think like a computer scientist, at least a little bit.

— *Ben Lauwens*

Why Julia?

Julia was originally released in 2012 by Alan Edelman, Stefan Karpinski, Jeff Bezanson, and Viral Shah. It is a free and open source programming language.

Choosing a programming language is always subjective. For me, the following characteristics of Julia are decisive:

- Julia is developed as a high-performance programming language.
- Julia uses multiple dispatch, which allows the programmer to choose from different programming patterns adapted to the application.
- Julia is a dynamically typed language that can easily be used interactively.
- Julia has a nice high-level syntax that is easy to learn.
- Julia is an optionally typed programming language whose (user-defined) data types make the code clearer and more robust.
- Julia has an extended standard library and numerous third-party packages are available.

Julia is a unique programming language because it solves the so-called "two languages problem." No other programming language is needed to write high-performance code. This does not mean it happens automatically. It is the responsibility of the programmer to optimize the code that forms a bottleneck, but this can done in Julia itself.

Who Is This Book For?

This book is for anyone who wants to learn to program. No formal prior knowledge is required.

New concepts are introduced gradually and more advanced topics are described in later chapters.

Think Julia can be used for a one-semester course at the high school or college level.

Conventions Used in This Book

The following typographical conventions are used in this book:

Italic
    Indicates new terms, URLs, email addresses, filenames, and file extensions.

`Constant width`

Used for program listings, as well as within paragraphs to refer to program elements such as variable or function names, databases, data types, environment variables, statements, and keywords.

`Constant width bold`

Shows commands or other text that should be typed literally by the user.

`Constant width italic`

Shows text that should be replaced with user-supplied values or by values determined by context.

This element signifies a tip or suggestion.

This element signifies a general note.

This element indicates a warning or caution.

Using Code Examples

All code used in this book is available from a Git repository on GitHub (*https://github.com/BenLauwens/ThinkJulia.jl*). If you are not familiar with Git, it is a version control system that allows you to keep track of the files that make up a project. A collection of files under Git's control is called a "repository." GitHub is a hosting service that provides storage for Git repositories and a convenient web interface.

A convenience package is provided that can be directly added to Julia. Just type **add https://github.com/BenLauwens/ThinkJulia.jl** in the REPL in Pkg mode, see "Turtles" on page 35.

The easiest way to run Julia code is by going to *https://juliabox.com* and starting a free session. Both the REPL and a notebook interface are available. If you want to have Julia locally installed on your computer, you can download JuliaPro (*https://juliacomputing.com/products/juliapro.html*) for free from Julia Computing. It consists of a recent Julia version, the Juno interactive development environment based on Atom, and a number of preinstalled Julia packages. If you are more adventurous, you can download Julia from *https://julialang.org*, install the editor you like (e.g., Atom or Visual Studio Code), and activate the plug-ins for Julia integration. To a local install, you can also add the IJulia package and run a Jupyter notebook on your computer.

This book is here to help you get your job done. In general, you may use example code in your programs and documentation. You do not need to contact us for permission unless you're reproducing a significant portion of the code. For example, writing a program that uses several chunks of code from this book does not require permission. Selling or distributing a CD-ROM of examples from O'Reilly books does require permission. Answering a question by citing this book and quoting example code does not require permission. Incorporating a significant amount of example code from this book into your product's documentation does require permission.

We appreciate, but do not require, attribution. An attribution usually includes the title, author, publisher, and ISBN. For example: "*Think Julia* by Ben Lauwens and Allen B. Downey (O'Reilly). Copyright 2019 Allen B. Downey, Ben Lauwens, 978-1-492-04503-8."

If you feel your use of code examples falls outside fair use or the permission given above, feel free to contact us at *permissions@oreilly.com*.

O'Reilly Online Learning

 For almost 40 years, *O'Reilly Media* has provided technology and business training, knowledge, and insight to help companies succeed.

Our unique network of experts and innovators share their knowledge and expertise through books, articles, conferences, and our online learning platform. O'Reilly's online learning platform gives you on-demand access to live training courses, in-depth learning paths, interactive coding environments, and a vast collection of text and video from O'Reilly and 200+ other publishers. For more information, please visit *http://oreilly.com*.

How to Contact Us

Please address comments and questions concerning this book to the publisher:

O'Reilly Media, Inc.
1005 Gravenstein Highway North
Sebastopol, CA 95472
800-998-9938 (in the United States or Canada)
707-829-0515 (international or local)
707-829-0104 (fax)

We have a web page for this book, where we list errata, examples, and any additional information. You can access this page at *https://oreil.ly/think-julia*.

To comment or ask technical questions about this book, please send an email to *book-questions@oreilly.com*.

For more information about our books, courses, conferences, and news, see our website at *http://www.oreilly.com*.

Find us on Facebook: *http://facebook.com/oreilly*

Follow us on Twitter: *http://twitter.com/oreillymedia*

Watch us on YouTube: *http://www.youtube.com/oreillymedia*

Acknowledgments

I really want to thank Allen for writing *Think Python* and allowing me to port his book to Julia. Your enthusiasm is contagious!

I would also like to thank the technical reviewers for this book, who made many helpful suggestions: Tim Besard, Bart Janssens, and David P. Sanders.

Thanks to Melissa Potter from O'Reilly Media, who made this a better book. You forced me to do things right and make this book as original as possible.

Thanks to Matt Hacker from O'Reilly Media, who helped me out with the Atlas toolchain and some syntax highlighting issues.

Thanks to all the students who worked with an early version of this book and all the contributors (listed below) who sent in corrections and suggestions.

Contributor List

If you have a suggestion or correction, please send email to *ben.lauwens@gmail.com* or open an issue on GitHub (*https://github.com/BenLauwens/ThinkJulia.jl*). If I make a change based on your feedback, I will add you to the contributor list (unless you ask to be omitted).

Let me know what version of the book you are working with, and what format. If you include at least part of the sentence the error appears in, that will make it easy for me to search. Page and section numbers are fine, too, but not quite as easy to work with. Thanks!

- Scott Jones pointed out the name change of `Void` to `Nothing`, and this started the migration to Julia v1.0.
- Robin Deits found some typos in Chapter 2.
- Mark Schmitz suggested turning on syntax highlighting.
- Zigu Zhao caught some bugs in Chapter 8.
- Oleg Soloviev caught an error in the URL to add the `ThinkJulia` package.
- Aaron Ang found some rendering and naming issues.
- Sergey Volkov caught a broken link in Chapter 7.
- Sean McAllister suggested mentioning the excellent package `BenchmarkTools`.
- Carlos Bolech sent a long list of corrections and suggestions.
- Krishna Kumar corrected the Markov example in Chapter 18.

CHAPTER 1

The Way of the Program

The goal of this book is to teach you to think like a computer scientist. This way of thinking combines some of the best features of mathematics, engineering, and natural science. Like mathematicians, computer scientists use formal languages to denote ideas (specifically computations). Like engineers, they design things, assembling components into systems and evaluating trade-offs among alternatives. Like scientists, they observe the behavior of complex systems, form hypotheses, and test predictions.

The single most important skill for a computer scientist is *problem solving*. Problem solving means the ability to formulate problems, think creatively about solutions, and express a solution clearly and accurately. As it turns out, the process of learning to program is an excellent opportunity to practice problem-solving skills. That's why this chapter is called "The Way of the Program."

On one level, you will be learning to program, a useful skill by itself. On another level, you will use programming as a means to an end. As we go along, that end will become clearer.

What Is a Program?

A *program* is a sequence of instructions that specifies how to perform a computation. The computation might be something mathematical, such as solving a system of equations or finding the roots of a polynomial, but it can also be a symbolic computation, such as searching for and replacing text in a document, or something graphical, like processing an image or playing a video.

The details look different in different languages, but a few basic instructions appear in just about every language:

Input
> Get data from the keyboard, a file, the network, or some other device.

Output
> Display data on the screen, save it in a file, send it over the network, etc.

Math
> Perform basic mathematical operations like addition and multiplication.

Conditional execution
> Check for certain conditions and run the appropriate code.

Repetition
> Perform some action repeatedly, usually with some variation.

Believe it or not, that's pretty much all there is to it. Every program you've ever used, no matter how complicated, is made up of instructions that look pretty much like these. So you can think of programming as the process of breaking a large, complex task into smaller and smaller subtasks until the subtasks are simple enough to be performed with one of these basic instructions.

Running Julia

One of the challenges of getting started with Julia is that you might have to install it and related software on your computer. If you are familiar with your operating system, and especially if you are comfortable with the command-line interface, you will have no trouble installing Julia. But for beginners, it can be painful to learn about system administration and programming at the same time.

To avoid that problem, I recommend that you start out running Julia in a browser. Later, when you are comfortable with Julia, I'll make suggestions for installing Julia on your computer.

In the browser, you can run Julia on JuliaBox (*https://www.juliabox.com*). No installation is required—just point your browser there, log in, and start computing (see Appendix B).

The Julia *REPL* (Read–Eval–Print Loop) is a program that reads and executes Julia code. You can start the REPL by opening a terminal on JuliaBox and typing **julia** on the command line. When it starts, you should see output like this:

```
           _       _ _(_)_      |  Documentation: https://docs.julialang.org
          (_)     | (_) (_)     |
           _ _   _| |_  __ _    |  Type "?" for help, "]?" for Pkg help.
          | | | | | | |/ _` |   |
          | | |_| | | | (_| |   |  Version 1.1.0 (2019-01-21)
         _/ |\__'_|_|_|\__'_|   |  Official https://julialang.org/ release
        |__/                    |

julia>
```

The first lines contain information about the REPL, so it might be different for you. But you should check that the version number is at least 1.0.0.

The last line is a *prompt* that indicates that the REPL is ready for you to enter code. If you type a line of code and hit Enter, the REPL displays the result:

```
julia> 1 + 1
2
```

Code snippets can be copied and pasted verbatim, including the julia> prompt and any output.

Now you're ready to get started. From here on, I assume that you know how to start the Julia REPL and run code.

The First Program

Traditionally, the first program you write in a new language is called "Hello, World!" because all it does is display the words "Hello, World!" In Julia, it looks like this:

```
julia> println("Hello, World!")
Hello, World!
```

This is an example of a *print statement*, although it doesn't actually print anything on paper. It displays a result on the screen.

The quotation marks in the program mark the beginning and end of the text to be displayed; they don't appear in the result.

The parentheses indicate that println is a function. We'll get to functions in Chapter 3.

Arithmetic Operators

After "Hello, World!" the next step is arithmetic. Julia provides *operators*, which are symbols that represent computations like addition and multiplication.

The operators +, -, and * perform addition, subtraction, and multiplication, as in the following examples:

```
julia> 40 + 2
42
julia> 43 - 1
42
julia> 6 * 7
42
```

The operator / performs division:

```
julia> 84 / 2
42.0
```

You might wonder why the result is 42.0 instead of 42. I'll explain in the next section.

Finally, the operator ^ performs exponentiation; that is, it raises a number to a power:

```
julia> 6^2 + 6
42
```

Values and Types

A *value* is one of the basic things a program works with, like a letter or a number. Some values we have seen so far are 2, 42.0, and "Hello, World!".

These values belong to different *types*: 2 is an *integer*, 42.0 is a *floating-point number*, and "Hello, World!" is a *string*, so called because the letters it contains are strung together.

If you are not sure what type a value has, the REPL can tell you:

```
julia> typeof(2)
Int64
julia> typeof(42.0)
Float64
julia> typeof("Hello, World!")
String
```

Integers belong to the type Int64, strings belong to String, and floating-point numbers belong to Float64.

What about values like "2" and "42.0"? They look like numbers, but they are in quotation marks like strings. These are strings too:

```
julia> typeof("2")
String
julia> typeof("42.0")
String
```

When you type a large integer, you might be tempted to use commas between groups of digits, as in 1,000,000. This is not a legal *integer* in Julia, but it is legal:

```
julia> 1,000,000
(1, 0, 0)
```

That's not what we expected at all! Julia parses `1,000,000` as a comma-separated sequence of integers. We'll learn more about this kind of sequence later.

You can get the expected result using `1_000_000`, however.

Formal and Natural Languages

Natural languages are the languages people speak, such as English, Spanish, and French. They were not designed by people (although people try to impose some order on them); they evolved naturally.

Formal languages are languages that are designed by people for specific applications. For example, the notation that mathematicians use is a formal language that is particularly good at denoting relationships among numbers and symbols. Chemists use a formal language to represent the chemical structure of molecules. And most importantly, programming languages are formal languages that have been designed to express computations.

Formal languages tend to have strict *syntax* rules that govern the structure of statements. For example, in mathematics the statement $3 + 3 = 6$ has correct syntax, but $3 + = 3\$6$ does not. In chemistry, H_2O is a syntactically correct formula, but $_2Zz$ is not.

Syntax rules come in two flavors: *tokens* and *structure*. Tokens are the basic elements of the language, such as words, numbers, and chemical elements. One of the problems with $3 + = 3\$6$ is that $ is not a legal token in mathematics (at least as far as I know). Similarly, $_2Zz$ is not legal because there is no element with the abbreviation Zz.

The second type of syntax rule pertains to the way tokens are combined. The equation $3 + = 3$ is illegal because even though + and = are legal tokens, you can't have one right after the other. Similarly, in a chemical formula the subscript comes after the element name, not before.

This is @ well-structured Engli$h sentence with invalid t*kens in it. This sentence all valid tokens has, but invalid structure with.

When you read a sentence in English or a statement in a formal language, you have to figure out the structure (although in a natural language you do this subconsciously). This process is called *parsing*.

Although formal and natural languages have many features in common—tokens, structure, and syntax—there are some differences:

Ambiguity
    Natural languages are full of ambiguity, which people deal with by using contextual clues and other information. Formal languages are designed to be nearly or

completely unambiguous, which means that any statement has exactly one meaning, regardless of context.

Redundancy

In order to make up for ambiguity and reduce misunderstandings, natural languages employ lots of redundancy. As a result, they are often verbose. Formal languages are less redundant and more concise.

Literalness

Natural languages are full of idiom and metaphor. If I say, "The penny dropped," there is probably no penny and nothing dropping (this idiom means that someone understood something after a period of confusion). Formal languages mean exactly what they say.

Because we all grow up speaking natural languages, it is sometimes hard to adjust to formal languages. The difference between formal and natural language is like the difference between poetry and prose, but more so:

Poetry

Words are used for their sounds as well as for their meaning, and the whole poem together creates an effect or emotional response. Ambiguity is not only common but often deliberate.

Prose

The literal meaning of words is more important, and the structure contributes more meaning. Prose is more amenable to analysis than poetry but still often ambiguous.

Programs

The meaning of a computer program is unambiguous and literal, and can be understood entirely by analysis of the tokens and structure.

Formal languages are more dense than natural languages, so it takes longer to read them. Also, the structure is important, so it is not always best to read from top to bottom, left to right. Instead, you'll learn to parse the program in your head, identifying the tokens and interpreting the structure. Finally, the details matter. Small errors in spelling and punctuation, which you can get away with in natural languages, can make a big difference in a formal language.

Debugging

Programmers make mistakes. For whimsical reasons, programming errors are called *bugs* and the process of tracking them down is called *debugging*.

Programming, and especially debugging, sometimes brings out strong emotions. If you are struggling with a difficult bug, you might feel angry, despondent, or embarrassed.

There is evidence that people naturally respond to computers as if they were people. When they work well, we think of them as teammates, and when they are obstinate or rude, we respond to them the same way we respond to rude, obstinate people.[1]

Preparing for these reactions might help you deal with them. One approach is to think of the computer as an employee with certain strengths, like speed and precision, and particular weaknesses, like lack of empathy and inability to grasp the big picture.

Your job is to be a good manager: find ways to take advantage of the strengths and mitigate the weaknesses. And find ways to use your emotions to engage with the problem, without letting your reactions interfere with your ability to work effectively.

Learning to debug can be frustrating, but it is a valuable skill that is useful for many activities beyond programming. At the end of each chapter there is a section, like this one, with my suggestions for debugging. I hope they help!

Glossary

problem solving
> The process of formulating a problem, finding a solution, and expressing it.

program
> A sequence of instructions that specifies a computation.

REPL
> A program that repeatedly reads input, executes it, and outputs results.

prompt
> Characters displayed by the REPL to indicate that it is ready to take input from the user.

print statement
> An instruction that causes the Julia REPL to display a value on the screen.

operator
> A symbol that represents a simple computation like addition, multiplication, or string concatenation.

---

1 Reeves, Byron, and Clifford Ivar Nass. 1996. "The Media Equation: How People Treat Computers, Television, and New Media Like Real People and Places." Chicago, IL: Center for the Study of Language and Information; New York: Cambridge University Press.

value
> A basic unit of data, like a number or string, that a program manipulates.

type
> A category of values. The types we have seen so far are integers (`Int64`), floating-point numbers (`Float64`), and strings (`String`).

integer
> A type that represents whole numbers.

floating-point
> A type that represents numbers with a decimal point.

string
> A type that represents sequences of characters.

natural language
> Any one of the languages that people speak that evolved naturally.

formal language
> Any one of the languages that people have designed for specific purposes, such as representing mathematical ideas or computer programs. All programming languages are formal languages.

syntax
> The rules that govern the structure of a program.

token
> One of the basic elements of the syntactic structure of a program, analogous to a word in a natural language.

structure
> The way tokens are combined.

parse
> To examine a program and analyze the syntactic structure.

bug
> An error in a program.

debugging
> The process of finding and correcting bugs.

Exercises

It is a good idea to read this book in front of a computer so you can try out the examples as you go.

Exercise 1-1

Whenever you are experimenting with a new feature, you should try to make mistakes. For example, in the "Hello, World!" program, what happens if you leave out one of the quotation marks? What if you leave out both? What if you spell `println` wrong?

This kind of experiment helps you remember what you read; it also helps when you are programming, because you get to know what the error messages mean. It is better to make mistakes now and on purpose rather than later and accidentally.

1. In a print statement, what happens if you leave out one of the parentheses, or both?

2. If you are trying to print a string, what happens if you leave out one of the quotation marks, or both?

3. You can use a minus sign to make a negative number like -2. What happens if you put a plus sign before a number? What about 2++2?

4. In math notation, leading zeros are okay, as in 02. What happens if you try this in Julia?

5. What happens if you have two values with no operator between them?

Exercise 1-2

Start the Julia REPL and use it as a calculator.

1. How many seconds are there in 42 minutes 42 seconds?

2. How many miles are there in 10 kilometers? Note that there are 1.61 kilometers in a mile.

3. If you run a 10-kilometer race in 37 minutes 48 seconds, what is your average pace (time per mile in minutes and seconds)? What is your average speed in miles per hour?

CHAPTER 2

Variables, Expressions, and Statements

One of the most powerful features of a programming language is the ability to manipulate *variables*. A variable is a name that refers to a value.

Assignment Statements

An *assignment statement* creates a new variable and gives it a value:

```
julia> message = "And now for something completely different"
"And now for something completely different"
julia> n = 17
17
julia> n_val = 3.141592653589793
3.141592653589793
```

This example makes three assignments. The first assigns a string to a new variable named `message`, the second assigns the integer 17 to `n`, and the third assigns the (approximate) value of π to `n_val` (**\pi TAB**).

A common way to represent variables on paper is to write the name of each with an arrow pointing to its value. This kind of figure is called a *state diagram* because it shows what state each of the variables is in (think of it as the variable's state of mind). Figure 2-1 shows the result of the previous example.

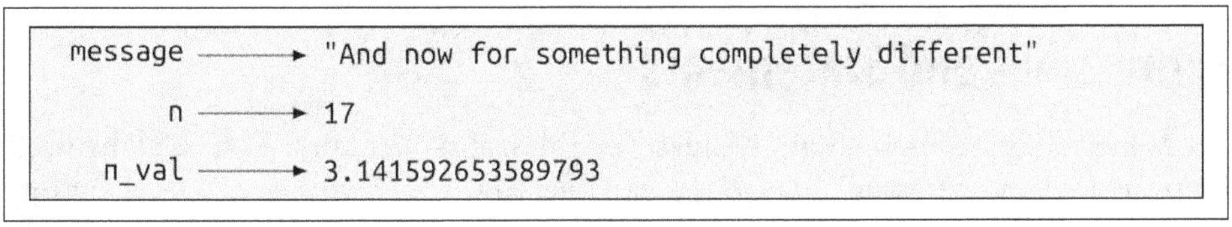

```
message ———▸ "And now for something completely different"
      n ———▸ 17
  n_val ———▸ 3.141592653589793
```

Figure 2-1. State diagram

Variable Names

Programmers generally choose names for their variables that are meaningful—they document what the variable is used for.

Variable names can be as long as you like. They can contain almost all Unicode characters (see "Characters" on page 87), but they can't begin with a number. It is legal to use uppercase letters, but it is conventional to use only lowercase for variable names.

Unicode characters can be entered via tab completion of LaTeX-like abbreviations in the Julia REPL.

The underscore character, _, can appear in a name. It is often used in names with multiple words, such as your_name or airspeed_of_unladen_swallow.

If you give a variable an illegal name, you get a syntax error:

```
julia> 76trombones = "big parade"
ERROR: syntax: "76" is not a valid function argument name
julia> more@ = 1000000
ERROR: syntax: extra token "@" after end of expression
julia> struct = "Advanced Theoretical Zymurgy"
ERROR: syntax: unexpected "="
```

76trombones is illegal because it begins with a number. more@ is illegal because it contains an illegal character, @. But what's wrong with struct?

It turns out that struct is one of Julia's *keywords*. The REPL uses keywords to recognize the structure of the program, and they cannot be used as variable names.

Julia has these keywords:

abstract type	baremodule	begin	break	catch
const	continue	do	else	elseif
end	export	finally	for	false
function	global	if	import	in
let	local	macro	module	mutable struct
primitive type	quote	return	true	try
using	struct	where	while	

You don't have to memorize this list. In most development environments, keywords are displayed in a different color; if you try to use one as a variable name, you'll know.

Expressions and Statements

An *expression* is a combination of values, variables, and operators. A value all by itself is considered an expression, and so is a variable, so the following are all legal expressions:

```
julia> 42
42
```

```
julia> n
17
julia> n + 25
42
```

When you type an expression at the prompt, the REPL *evaluates* it, which means that it finds the value of the expression. In this example, n has the value 17 and n + 25 has the value 42.

A *statement* is a unit of code that has an effect, like creating a variable or displaying a value:

```
julia> n = 17
17
julia> println(n)
17
```

The first line here is an assignment statement that gives a value to n. The second line is a print statement that displays the value of n.

When you type a statement, the REPL *executes* it, which means that it does whatever the statement says.

Script Mode

So far we have run Julia in *interactive mode*, which means that you interact directly with the REPL. Interactive mode is a good way to get started, but if you are working with more than a few lines of code, it can be clumsy.

The alternative is to save code in a file called a *script* and then run Julia in *script mode* to execute the script. By convention, Julia scripts have names that end with *.jl*.

If you know how to create and run a script on your computer, you are ready to go. Otherwise I recommend using JuliaBox again. Open a text file, write the script, and save the file with a *.jl* extension. The script can be executed in a terminal with the command **julia *name_of_the_script*.jl**.

Because Julia provides both modes, you can test bits of code in interactive mode before you put them in a script. But there are differences between interactive mode and script mode that can be confusing.

For example, if you are using Julia as a calculator, you might type:

```
julia> miles = 26.2
26.2
julia> miles * 1.61
42.182
```

The first line assigns a value to `miles` and displays the value. The second line is an expression, so the REPL evaluates it and displays the result. It turns out that a marathon is about 42 kilometers.

But if you type the same code into a script and run it, you get no output at all. In script mode an expression, all by itself, has no visible effect. Julia actually evaluates the expression, but it doesn't display the value unless you tell it to:

```
miles = 26.2
println(miles * 1.61)
```

This behavior can be confusing at first.

A script usually contains a sequence of statements. If there is more than one statement, the results appear one at a time as the statements execute.

For example, the script:

```
println(1)
x = 2
println(x)
```

produces the output:

```
1
2
```

The assignment statement produces no output.

Exercise 2-1

To check your understanding, type the following statements in the Julia REPL and see what they do:

```
5
x = 5
x + 1
```

Now put the same statements in a script and run it. What is the output? Modify the script by transforming each expression into a print statement and then run it again.

Operator Precedence

When an expression contains more than one operator, the order of evaluation depends on the *operator precedence*. For mathematical operators, Julia follows mathematical convention. The acronym *PEMDAS* is a useful way to remember the rules:

- *Parentheses* have the highest precedence and can be used to force an expression to evaluate in the order you want. Since expressions in parentheses are evaluated first, `2*(3-1)` is 4, and `(1+1)^(5-2)` is 8. You can also use parentheses to make an

---

expression easier to read, as in (minute * 100) / 60, even if it doesn't change the result.

- *Exponentiation* has the next highest precedence, so 1+2^3 is 9, not 27, and 2*3^2 is 18, not 36.

- *Multiplication* and *Division* have higher precedence than *Addition* and *Subtraction*. So, 2*3-1 is 5, not 4, and 6+4/2 is 8, not 5.

- Operators with the same precedence are evaluated from left to right (except exponentiation). So in the expression degrees / 2 * π, the division happens first and the result is multiplied by π. To divide by 2π, you can use parentheses, or write degrees / 2 / π or degrees / 2π.

 I don't work very hard to remember the precedence of operators. If I can't tell by looking at the expression, I use parentheses to make it obvious.

String Operations

In general, you can't perform mathematical operations on strings, even if the strings look like numbers, so the following are illegal:

```
"2" - "1"    "eggs" / "easy"    "third" + "a charm"
```

But there are two exceptions, * and ^.

The * operator performs *string concatenation*, which means it joins the strings by linking them end-to-end. For example:

```
julia> first_str = "throat"
"throat"
julia> second_str = "warbler"
"warbler"
julia> first_str * second_str
"throatwarbler"
```

The ^ operator also works on strings; it performs repetition. For example, "Spam"^3 is "SpamSpamSpam". If one of the values is a string, the other has to be an integer.

This use of * and ^ makes sense by analogy with multiplication and exponentiation. Just as 4^3 is equivalent to 4*4*4, we expect "Spam"^3 to be the same as "Spam"*"Spam"*"Spam", and it is.

Comments

As programs get bigger and more complicated, they get more difficult to read. Formal languages are dense, and it is often difficult to look at a piece of code and figure out what it is doing, or why.

For this reason, it is a good idea to add notes to your programs to explain in natural language what the program is doing. These notes are called *comments*, and they start with the # symbol:

```
# compute the percentage of the hour that has elapsed
percentage = (minute * 100) / 60
```

In this case, the comment appears on a line by itself. You can also put comments at the end of a line:

```
percentage = (minute * 100) / 60   # percentage of an hour
```

Everything from the # to the end of the line is ignored—it has no effect on the execution of the program.

Comments are most useful when they document nonobvious features of the code. It is reasonable to assume that the reader can figure out *what* the code does; it is more useful to explain *why*.

This comment is redundant with the code and useless:

```
v = 5   # assign 5 to v
```

This comment contains useful information that is not in the code:

```
v = 5   # velocity in meters/second
```

 Good variable names can reduce the need for comments, but long names can make complex expressions hard to read, so there is a trade-off.

Debugging

Three kinds of errors can occur in a program: syntax errors, runtime errors, and semantic errors. It is useful to distinguish between them in order to track them down more quickly:

Syntax error
> "Syntax" refers to the structure of a program and the rules about that structure. For example, parentheses have to come in matching pairs, so (1 + 2) is legal, but 8) is a syntax error.

If there is a syntax error anywhere in your program, Julia displays an error message and quits, and you will not be able to run the program. During the first few weeks of your programming career, you might spend a lot of time tracking down syntax errors. As you gain experience, you will make fewer errors and find them faster.

Runtime error

The second type of error is a runtime error, so called because the error does not appear until after the program has started running. These errors are also called *exceptions* because they usually indicate that something exceptional (and bad) has happened.

Runtime errors are rare in the simple programs you will see in the first few chapters, so it might be a while before you encounter one.

Semantic error

The third type of error is "semantic," which means related to meaning. If there is a semantic error in your program, it will run without generating error messages, but it will not do the right thing. It will do something else. Specifically, it will do what you told it to do.

Identifying semantic errors can be tricky because it requires you to work backward by looking at the output of the program and trying to figure out what it is doing.

Glossary

variable

A name that refers to a value.

assignment

A statement that assigns a value to a variable.

state diagram

A graphical representation of a set of variables and the values they refer to.

keyword

A reserved word that is used to parse a program; you cannot use keywords like `if`, `function`, and `while` as variable names.

expression

A combination of variables, operators, and values that represents a single result.

evaluate

To simplify an expression by performing the operations in order to yield a single value.

statement

A section of code that represents a command or action. So far, the statements we have seen are assignments and print statements.

execute

To run a statement and do what it says.

interactive mode

A way of using the Julia REPL by typing code at the prompt.

script mode

A way of using Julia to read code from a script and run it.

script

A program stored in a file.

operator precedence

Rules governing the order in which expressions involving multiple mathematical operators and operands are evaluated.

concatenate

To join two strings end-to-end.

comment

Information in a program that is meant for other programmers (or anyone reading the source code) and has no effect on the execution of the program.

syntax error

An error in a program that makes it impossible to parse (and therefore impossible to interpret).

runtime error or exception

An error that is detected while the program is running.

semantics

The meaning of a program.

semantic error

An error in a program that makes it do something other than what the programmer intended.

Exercises

Exercise 2-2

Repeating my advice from the previous chapter, whenever you learn a new feature, you should try it out in interactive mode and make errors on purpose to see what goes wrong.

1. We've seen that n = 42 is legal. What about 42 = n?
2. How about x = y = 1?
3. In some languages every statement ends with a semicolon, ;. What happens if you put a semicolon at the end of a Julia statement?
4. What if you put a period at the end of a statement?
5. In math notation you can multiply x and y like this: x y. What happens if you try that in Julia? What about 5x?

Exercise 2-3

Practice using the Julia REPL as a calculator:

1. The volume of a sphere with radius r is $\frac{4}{3}\pi r^3$. What is the volume of a sphere with radius 5?
2. Suppose the cover price of a book is $24.95, but bookstores get a 40% discount. Shipping costs $3 for the first copy and 75 cents for each additional copy. What is the total wholesale cost for 60 copies?
3. If I leave my house at 6:52 a.m. and run 1 mile at an easy pace (8:15 per mile), then 3 miles at tempo (7:12 per mile) and 1 mile at easy pace again, what time do I get home for breakfast?

CHAPTER 3

Functions

In the context of programming, a *function* is a named sequence of statements that performs a computation. When you define a function, you specify the name and the sequence of statements. Later, you can "call" the function by name.

Function Calls

We have already seen one example of a function call:

```
julia> println("Hello, World!")
Hello, World!
```

The name of the function is `println`. The expression in parentheses is called the *argument* of the function.

It is common to say that a function "takes" an argument and "returns" a result. The result is also called the *return value*.

Julia provides functions that convert values from one type to another. The `parse` function takes a string and converts it to any number type, if it can, or complains otherwise:

```
julia> parse(Int64, "32")
32
julia> parse(Float64, "3.14159")
3.14159
julia> parse(Int64, "Hello")
ERROR: ArgumentError: invalid base 10 digit 'H' in "Hello"
```

`trunc` can convert floating-point values to integers, but it doesn't round off; it chops off the fraction part:

```
julia> trunc(Int64, 3.99999)
3
```

```
julia> trunc(Int64, -2.3)
-2
```

`float` converts integers to floating-point numbers:

```
julia> float(32)
32.0
```

Finally, `string` converts its argument to a string:

```
julia> string(32)
"32"
julia> string(3.14159)
"3.14159"
```

Math Functions

In Julia, most of the familiar mathematical functions are directly available. The following example uses `log10` to compute a signal-to-noise ratio in decibels (assuming that `signal_power` and `noise_power` are defined). `log`, which computes natural logarithms, is also provided:

```
ratio = signal_power / noise_power
decibels = 10 * log10(ratio)
```

This next example finds the sine of `radians`. The name of the variable is a hint that `sin` and the other trigonometric functions (`cos`, `tan`, etc.) take arguments in radians:

```
radians = 0.7
height = sin(radians)
```

To convert from degrees to radians, divide by 180 and multiply by π:

```
julia> degrees = 45
45
julia> radians = degrees / 180 * π
0.7853981633974483
julia> sin(radians)
0.7071067811865475
```

The value of the variable `π` is a floating-point approximation of π, accurate to about 16 digits.

If you know trigonometry, you can check the previous result by comparing it to the square root of 2 divided by 2:

```
julia> sqrt(2) / 2
0.7071067811865476
```

Composition

So far, we have looked at the elements of a program—variables, expressions, and statements—in isolation, without talking about how to combine them.

One of the most useful features of programming languages is their ability to take small building blocks and *compose* them. For example, the argument of a function can be any kind of expression, including arithmetic operators:

```
x = sin(degrees / 360 * 2 * n)
```

and even function calls:

```
x = exp(log(x+1))
```

Almost anywhere you can put a value, you can put an arbitrary expression, with one exception: the left side of an assignment statement has to be a variable name. We'll see exceptions to this later, but as a general rule any other expression on the left side is a syntax error:

```
julia> minutes = hours * 60 # right
120
julia> hours * 60 = minutes # wrong!
ERROR: syntax: "60" is not a valid function argument name
```

Adding New Functions

So far, we have only been using the functions that come with Julia, but it is also possible to add new functions. A *function definition* specifies the name of a new function and the sequence of statements that run when the function is called. Here is an example:

```
function printlyrics()
    println("I'm a lumberjack, and I'm okay.")
    println("I sleep all night and I work all day.")
end
```

`function` is a keyword that indicates that this is a function definition. The name of the function is `printlyrics`. The rules for function names are the same as for variable names: they can contain almost all Unicode characters (see "Characters" on page 87), but the first character can't be a number. You can't use a keyword as the name of a function, and you should avoid having a variable and a function with the same name.

The empty parentheses after the name indicate that this function doesn't take any arguments.

The first line of the function definition is called the *header*; the rest is called the *body*. The body is terminated with the keyword `end`, and it can contain any number of statements. For readability the body of the function should be indented.

The quotation marks must be "straight quotes," usually located next to Enter on the keyboard. "Curly quotes," like the ones in this sentence, are not legal in Julia.

If you type a function definition in interactive mode, the REPL indents to let you know that the definition isn't complete:

```
julia> function printlyrics()
          println("I'm a lumberjack, and I'm okay.")
```

To end the function, you have to enter end.

The syntax for calling the new function is the same as for built-in functions:

```
julia> printlyrics()
I'm a lumberjack, and I'm okay.
I sleep all night and I work all day.
```

Once you have defined a function, you can use it inside another function. For example, to repeat the previous refrain, we could write a function called repeatlyrics:

```
function repeatlyrics()
    printlyrics()
    printlyrics()
end
```

And then call repeatlyrics:

```
julia> repeatlyrics()
I'm a lumberjack, and I'm okay.
I sleep all night and I work all day.
I'm a lumberjack, and I'm okay.
I sleep all night and I work all day.
```

But that's not really how the song goes.

Definitions and Uses

Pulling together the code fragments from the previous section, the whole program looks like this:

```
function printlyrics()
    println("I'm a lumberjack, and I'm okay.")
    println("I sleep all night and I work all day.")
end

function repeatlyrics()
    printlyrics()
    printlyrics()
end

repeatlyrics()
```

This program contains two function definitions: `printlyrics` and `repeatlyrics`. Function definitions get executed just like other statements, but the effect is to create *function objects*. The statements inside the function do not run until the function is called, and the function definition generates no output.

As you might expect, you have to create a function before you can run it. In other words, the function definition has to run before the function gets called.

Exercise 3-1

Restart the REPL and move the last line of this program to the top, so the function call appears before the definitions. Run the program and see what error message you get.

Now move the function call back to the bottom and move the definition of `printlyrics` after the definition of `repeatlyrics`. What happens when you run this program?

Flow of Execution

To ensure that a function is defined before its first use, you have to know the order statements run in, which is called the *flow of execution*.

Execution always begins at the first statement of the program. Statements are run one at a time, in order, from top to bottom.

Function definitions do not alter the flow of execution of the program, but remember that statements inside a function don't run until the function is called.

A function call is like a detour in the flow of execution. Instead of going to the next statement, the flow jumps to the body of the function, runs the statements there, and then comes back to pick up where it left off.

That sounds simple enough, until you remember that one function can call another. While in the middle of one function, the program might have to run the statements in another function. Then, while running that new function, the program might have to run yet another function!

Fortunately, Julia is good at keeping track of where it is, so each time a function completes, the program picks up where it left off in the function that called it. When it gets to the end of the program, it terminates.

In summary, when you read a program, you don't always want to read from top to bottom. Sometimes it makes more sense if you follow the flow of execution.

Parameters and Arguments

Some of the functions we have seen require arguments. For example, when you call sin you pass a number as an argument. Some functions take more than one argument: parse takes two, a number type and a string.

Inside the function, the arguments are assigned to variables called *parameters*. Here is a definition for a function that takes an argument:

```
function printtwice(bruce)
    println(bruce)
    println(bruce)
end
```

This function assigns the argument to a parameter named bruce. When the function is called, it prints the value of the parameter (whatever it is) twice.

This function works with any value that can be printed:

```
julia> printtwice("Spam")
Spam
Spam
julia> printtwice(42)
42
42
julia> printtwice(π)
π = 3.1415926535897...
π = 3.1415926535897...
```

The same rules of composition that apply to built-in functions also apply to programmer-defined functions, so we can use any kind of expression as an argument for printtwice:

```
julia> printtwice("Spam "^4)
Spam Spam Spam Spam
Spam Spam Spam Spam
julia> printtwice(cos(π))
-1.0
-1.0
```

The argument is evaluated before the function is called, so in these examples the expressions "Spam "^4 and cos(π) are only evaluated once.

You can also use a variable as an argument:

```
julia> michael = "Eric, the half a bee."
"Eric, the half a bee."
julia> printtwice(michael)
Eric, the half a bee.
Eric, the half a bee.
```

The name of the variable we pass as an argument (michael) has nothing to do with the name of the parameter (bruce). It doesn't matter what the value was called back home (in the caller); here in printtwice, we call everybody bruce.

Variables and Parameters Are Local

When you create a variable inside a function, it is *local*, which means that it only exists inside the function. For example:

```
function cattwice(part1, part2)
    concat = part1 * part2
    printtwice(concat)
end
```

This function takes two arguments, concatenates them, and prints the result twice. Here is an example that uses it:

```
julia> line1 = "Bing tiddle "
"Bing tiddle "
julia> line2 = "tiddle bang."
"tiddle bang."
julia> cattwice(line1, line2)
Bing tiddle tiddle bang.
Bing tiddle tiddle bang.
```

When cattwice terminates, the variable concat is destroyed. If we try to print it, we get an exception:

```
julia> println(concat)
ERROR: UndefVarError: concat not defined
```

Parameters are also local. For example, outside printtwice, there is no such thing as bruce.

Stack Diagrams

To keep track of which variables can be used where, it is sometimes useful to draw a *stack diagram*. Like state diagrams, stack diagrams show the value of each variable, but they also show the function each variable belongs to.

Each function is represented by a *frame*. A frame is a box with the name of a function beside it and the parameters and variables of the function inside it. The stack diagram for the previous example is shown in Figure 3-1.

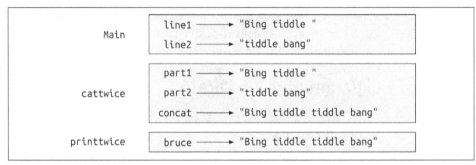

Figure 3-1. Stack diagram

The frames are arranged in a stack that indicates which function called which. In this example, printtwice was called by cattwice, and cattwice was called by Main, which is a special name for the topmost frame. When you create a variable outside of any function, it belongs to Main.

Each parameter refers to the same value as its corresponding argument. So, part1 has the same value as line1, part2 has the same value as line2, and bruce has the same value as concat.

If an error occurs during a function call, Julia prints the name of the function, the name of the function that called it, and the name of the function that called *that*, all the way back to Main.

For example, if you try to access concat from within printtwice, you get an UndefVarError:

```
ERROR: UndefVarError: concat not defined
Stacktrace:
 [1] printtwice at ./REPL[1]:2 [inlined]
 [2] cattwice(::String, ::String) at ./REPL[2]:3
```

This list of functions is called a *stacktrace*. It tells you what program file the error occurred in, and what line, and what functions were executing at the time. It also shows the line of code that caused the error.

The order of the functions in the stacktrace is the inverse of the order of the frames in the stack diagram. The function that is currently running is at the top.

Fruitful Functions and Void Functions

Some of the functions we have used, such as the math functions, return results; for lack of a better name, I call them *fruitful functions*. Other functions, like printtwice, perform an action but don't return a value. They are called *void functions*.

When you call a fruitful function, you almost always want to do something with the result. For example, you might assign it to a variable or use it as part of an expression:

```
x = cos(radians)
golden = (sqrt(5) + 1) / 2
```

When you call a function in interactive mode, Julia displays the result:

```
julia> sqrt(5)
2.23606797749979
```

But in a script, if you call a fruitful function all by itself, the return value is lost forever!

```
sqrt(5)
```

This script computes the square root of 5, but since it doesn't store or display the result, it is not very useful.

Void functions might display something on the screen or have some other effect, but they don't have a return value. If you assign the result to a variable, you get a special value called nothing:

```
julia> result = printtwice("Bing")
Bing
Bing
julia> show(result)
nothing
```

To print the value nothing, you have to use the function show, which is like print but can handle this special value.

The value nothing is not the same as the string "nothing". It is a special value that has its own type:

```
julia> typeof(nothing)
Nothing
```

The functions we have written so far are all void. We will start writing fruitful functions in a few chapters.

Why Functions?

It may not be clear why it is worth the trouble to divide a program into functions. There are several reasons:

- Creating a new function gives you an opportunity to name a group of statements, which makes your program easier to read and debug.
- Functions can make a program smaller by eliminating repetitive code. Later, if you make a change, you only have to make it in one place.

- Dividing a long program into functions allows you to debug the parts one at a time and then assemble them into a working whole.
- Well-designed functions are often useful for many programs. Once you write and debug one, you can reuse it.
- In Julia, functions can improve performance a lot.

Debugging

One of the most important skills you will acquire is debugging. Although it can be frustrating, debugging is one of the most intellectually rich, challenging, and interesting parts of programming.

In some ways debugging is like detective work. You are confronted with clues and you have to infer the processes and events that led to the results you see.

Debugging is also like an experimental science. Once you have an idea about what is going wrong, you modify your program and try again. If your hypothesis was correct, you can predict the result of the modification, and you take a step closer to a working program. If your hypothesis was wrong, you have to come up with a new one. As Sherlock Holmes pointed out,

> When you have eliminated the impossible, whatever remains, however improbable, must be the truth.
>
> —A. Conan Doyle, *The Sign of Four*

For some people, programming and debugging are the same thing. That is, programming is the process of gradually debugging a program until it does what you want. The idea is that you should start with a working program and make small modifications, debugging them as you go.

For example, Linux is an operating system that contains millions of lines of code, but it started out as a simple program Linus Torvalds used to explore the Intel 80386 chip. According to Larry Greenfield in *The Linux Users' Guide* (version beta-1), "One of Linus's earlier projects was a program that would switch between printing AAAA and BBBB. This later evolved to Linux."

Glossary

function
A named sequence of statements that performs some useful operation. Functions may or may not take arguments and may or may not produce a result.

function call
> A statement that runs a function. It consists of the function name followed by an argument list in parentheses.

argument
> A value provided to a function when the function is called. This value is assigned to the corresponding parameter in the function.

return value
> The result of a function. If a function call is used as an expression, the return value is the value of the expression.

composition
> Using an expression as part of a larger expression, or a statement as part of a larger statement.

function definition
> A statement that creates a new function, specifying its name, parameters, and the statements it contains.

header
> The first line of a function definition.

body
> The sequence of statements inside a function definition.

function object
> A value created by a function definition. The name of the function is a variable that refers to a function object.

flow of execution
> The order statements run in.

parameter
> A name used inside a function to refer to the value passed as an argument.

local variable
> A variable defined inside a function. A local variable can only be used inside its function.

stack diagram
> A graphical representation of a stack of functions, their variables, and the values they refer to.

frame
> A box in a stack diagram that represents a function call. It contains the local variables and parameters of the function.

stacktrace
A list of the functions that are executing, printed when an exception occurs.

fruitful function
A function that returns a value.

void function
A function that always returns `nothing`.

nothing
A special value returned by void functions.

Exercises

These exercises should be done using only the statements and other features introduced so far.

Exercise 3-2

Write a function named `rightjustify` that takes a string named s as a parameter and prints the string with enough leading spaces so that the last letter of the string is in column 70 of the display:

```
julia> rightjustify("monty")
                                                                 monty
```

Use string concatenation and repetition. Also, Julia provides a built-in function called `length` that returns the length of a string, so the value of `length("monty")` is 5.

Exercise 3-3

A function object is a value you can assign to a variable or pass as an argument. For example, `dotwice` is a function that takes a function object as an argument and calls it twice:

```
function dotwice(f)
    f()
    f()
end
```

Here's an example that uses `dotwice` to call a function named `printspam` twice:

```
function printspam()
    println("spam")
end

dotwice(printspam)
```

1. Type this example into a script and test it.

2. Modify dotwice so that it takes two arguments, a function object and a value, and calls the function twice, passing the value as an argument.

3. Copy the definition of printtwice from earlier in this chapter to your script.

4. Use the modified version of dotwice to call printtwice twice, passing "spam" as an argument.

5. Define a new function called dofour that takes a function object and a value and calls the function four times, passing the value as a parameter. There should be only two statements in the body of this function, not four.

Exercise 3-4

1. Write a function printgrid that draws a grid like the following:

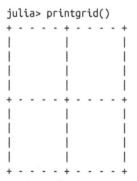

```
julia> printgrid()
+ - - - - + - - - - +
|         |         |
|         |         |
|         |         |
|         |         |
+ - - - - + - - - - +
|         |         |
|         |         |
|         |         |
|         |         |
+ - - - - + - - - - +
```

2. Write a function that draws a similar grid with four rows and four columns.

Credit: This exercise is based on an exercise in *Practical C Programming*, by Steve Oualline (O'Reilly).

To print more than one value on a line, you can print a comma-separated sequence of values:

```
println("+", "-")
```

The function `print` does not advance to the next line:

```
print("+ ")
println("-")
```

The output of these statements is "+ -" on the same line. The output from the next print statement would begin on the next line.

CHAPTER 4

Case Study: Interface Design

This chapter presents a case study that demonstrates a process for designing functions that work together.

It introduces turtle graphics, a way to create programmatic drawings. Turtle graphics are not included in the standard library, so to use them you'll have to add the `ThinkJulia` module to your Julia setup.

The examples in this chapter can be executed in a graphical notebook on JuliaBox, which combines code, formatted text, math, and multimedia in a single document (see Appendix B).

Turtles

A *module* is a file that contains a collection of related functions. Julia provides some modules in its standard library. Additional functionality can be added from a growing collection of *packages* (*https://juliaobserver.com*).

Packages can be installed in the REPL by entering the Pkg REPL mode using the key] and using the `add` command:

```
(v1.0) pkg> add https://github.com/BenLauwens/ThinkJulia.jl
```

This can take some time.

Before we can use the functions in a module, we have to import it with a *using statement*:

```
julia> using ThinkJulia

julia> 🐢 = Turtle()
Luxor.Turtle(0.0, 0.0, true, 0.0, (0.0, 0.0, 0.0))
```

The `ThinkJulia` module provides a function called `Turtle` that creates a `Luxor.Turtle` object, which we assign to a variable named 🐢(`\:turtle: TAB`).

Once you create a turtle, you can call a function to move it around. For example, to move the turtle forward:

```
@svg begin
    forward(🐢, 100)
end
```

The `@svg` keyword runs a macro that draws an SVG picture (Figure 4-1). Macros are an important but advanced feature of Julia.

```
┌─────────────────────────────────────────────┐
│                    ─────────                  │
└─────────────────────────────────────────────┘
```

Figure 4-1. Moving the turtle forward

The arguments of `forward` are the turtle and a distance in pixels, so the actual size of the line that's drawn depends on your display.

 Each turtle is holding a pen, which is either down or up; if the pen is down (the default), the turtle leaves a trail when it moves. Figure 4-1 shows the trail left behind by the turtle. To move the turtle without drawing a line, first call the function `penup`. To start drawing again, call `pendown`.

Another function you can call with a turtle as an argument is `turn` for turning. The second argument for `turn` is an angle in degrees.

To draw a right angle, modify the macro call:

```
🐢 = Turtle()
@svg begin
    forward(🐢, 100)
    turn(🐢, -90)
    forward(🐢, 100)
end
```

Exercise 4-1

Now modify the macro to draw a square. Don't go on until you've got it working!

Simple Repetition

Chances are you wrote something like this:

```
🐢 = Turtle()
@svg begin
    forward(🐢, 100)
```

```
        turn(🐢, -90)
        forward(🐢, 100)
        turn(🐢, -90)
        forward(🐢, 100)
        turn(🐢, -90)
        forward(🐢, 100)
    end
```

We can do the same thing more concisely with a for statement:

```
julia> for i in 1:4
           println("Hello!")
       end
Hello!
Hello!
Hello!
Hello!
```

This is the simplest use of the for statement; we will see more later. But that should be enough to let you rewrite your square-drawing program. Don't go on until you do.

Here is a for statement that draws a square:

```
🐢 = Turtle()
@svg begin
    for i in 1:4
        forward(🐢, 100)
        turn(🐢, -90)
    end
end
```

The syntax of a for statement is similar to a function definition. It has a header and a body that ends with the keyword end. The body can contain any number of statements.

A for statement is also called a *loop* because the flow of execution runs through the body and then loops back to the top. In this case, it runs the body four times.

This version is actually a little different from the previous square-drawing code because it makes another turn after drawing the last side of the square. The extra turn takes more time, but it simplifies the code if we do the same thing every time through the loop. This version also has the effect of leaving the turtle back in the starting position, facing in the starting direction.

Exercises

The following is a series of exercises using turtles. They are meant to be fun, but they have a point, too. While you are working on them, think about what the point is.

The following sections contain solutions to the exercises, so don't look until you have finished (or at least tried them).

Exercise 4-2

Write a function called `square` that takes a parameter named `t`, which is a turtle. It should use the turtle to draw a square.

Exercise 4-3

Write a function call that passes as an argument to `square`, and then run the macro again.

Exercise 4-4

Add another parameter, named `len`, to `square`. Modify the body so the length of the sides is `len`, and then modify the function call to provide a second argument. Run the macro again. Test with a range of values for `len`.

Exercise 4-5

Make a copy of `square` and change the name to `polygon`. Add another parameter named `n` and modify the body so it draws an *n*-sided regular polygon.

The exterior angles of an *n*-sided regular polygon are $\frac{360}{n}$ degrees.

Exercise 4-6

Write a function called `circle` that takes a turtle, `t`, and radius, `r`, as parameters and that draws an approximate circle by calling `polygon` with an appropriate length and number of sides. Test your function with a range of values of `r`.

Figure out the circumference of the circle and make sure that `len * n == circumference`.

Exercise 4-7

Make a more general version of `circle` called `arc` that takes an additional parameter `angle`, which determines what fraction of a circle to draw. `angle` is in units of degrees, so when `angle = 360`, `arc` should draw a complete circle.

Encapsulation

The first exercise asks you to put your square-drawing code into a function definition and then call the function, passing the turtle as a parameter. Here is a solution:

```
function square(t)
    for i in 1:4
        forward(t, 100)
        turn(t, -90)
    end
end
🐢 = Turtle()
@svg begin
    square(🐢)
end
```

The innermost statements, `forward` and `turn`, are indented twice to show that they are inside the `for` loop, which is inside the function definition.

Inside the function, `t` refers to the same turtle 🐢, so `turn(t, -90)` has the same effect as `turn(🐢, -90)`. In that case, why not call the parameter 🐢? The idea is that `t` can be any turtle, not just 🐢 so you could create a second turtle and pass it as an argument to `square`:

```
🐪 = Turtle()
@svg begin
    square(🐪)
end
```

Wrapping a piece of code up in a function is called *encapsulation*. One of the benefits of encapsulation is that it attaches a name to the code, which serves as a kind of documentation. Another advantage is that if you reuse the code, it is more concise to call a function twice than to copy and paste the body!

Generalization

The next step is to add a `len` parameter to `square`. Here is a solution:

```
function square(t, len)
    for i in 1:4
        forward(t, len)
        turn(t, -90)
    end
```

```
    end
🐢 = Turtle()
@svg begin
    square(🐢, 100)
end
```

Adding a parameter to a function is called *generalization* because it makes the function more general. In the previous version, the square is always the same size; in this version it can be any size.

The next step is also a generalization. Instead of drawing squares, polygon draws regular polygons with any number of sides. Here is a solution:

```
function polygon(t, n, len)
    angle = 360 / n
    for i in 1:n
        forward(t, len)
        turn(t, -angle)
    end
end
🐢 = Turtle()
@svg begin
    polygon(🐢, 7, 70)
end
```

This example draws a 7-sided polygon with side length 70.

Interface Design

The next step is to write circle, which takes a radius, r, as a parameter. Here is a simple solution that uses polygon to draw a 50-sided polygon:

```
function circle(t, r)
    circumference = 2 * π * r
    n = 50
    len = circumference / n
    polygon(t, n, len)
end
```

The first line computes the circumference of a circle with radius r using the formula 2πr. n is the number of line segments in our approximation of a circle, so len is the length of each segment. Thus, polygon draws a 50-sided polygon that approximates a circle with radius r.

One limitation of this solution is that n is a constant, which means that for very big circles, the line segments are too long, and for small circles, we waste time drawing very small segments. One solution would be to generalize the function by taking n as a parameter. This would give the user (whoever calls circle) more control, but the interface would be less clean.

The *interface* of a function is a summary of how it is used: What are the parameters? What does the function do? And what is the return value? An interface is "clean" if it allows the caller to do what he wants without dealing with unnecessary details.

In this example, r belongs in the interface because it specifies the circle to be drawn. n is less appropriate because it pertains to the details of how the circle should be rendered.

Rather than cluttering up the interface, it is better to choose an appropriate value of n depending on circumference:

```
function circle(t, r)
    circumference = 2 * n * r
    n = trunc(circumference / 3) + 3
    len = circumference / n
    polygon(t, n, len)
end
```

Now the number of segments is an integer near circumference/3, so the length of each segment is approximately 3, which is small enough that the circles look good but big enough to be efficient, and acceptable for any size circle.

Adding 3 to n guarantees that the polygon has at least three sides.

Refactoring

When I wrote circle, I was able to reuse polygon because a many-sided polygon is a good approximation of a circle. But arc is not as cooperative; we can't use polygon or circle to draw an arc.

One alternative is to start with a copy of polygon and transform it into arc. The result might look like this:

```
function arc(t, r, angle)
    arc_len = 2 * n * r * angle / 360
    n = trunc(arc_len / 3) + 1
    step_len = arc_len / n
    step_angle = angle / n
    for i in 1:n
        forward(t, step_len)
        turn(t, -step_angle)
    end
end
```

The second half of this function looks like polygon, but we can't reuse polygon without changing the interface. We could generalize polygon to take an angle as a third argument, but then polygon would no longer be an appropriate name! Instead, let's call the more general function polyline:

```
function polyline(t, n, len, angle)
    for i in 1:n
        forward(t, len)
        turn(t, -angle)
    end
end
```

Now we can rewrite `polygon` and `arc` to use `polyline`:

```
function polygon(t, n, len)
    angle = 360 / n
    polyline(t, n, len, angle)
end

function arc(t, r, angle)
    arc_len = 2 * n * r * angle / 360
    n = trunc(arc_len / 3) + 1
    step_len = arc_len / n
    step_angle = angle / n
    polyline(t, n, step_len, step_angle)
end
```

Finally, we can rewrite `circle` to use `arc`:

```
function circle(t, r)
    arc(t, r, 360)
end
```

This process—rearranging a program to improve interfaces and facilitate code reuse —is called *refactoring*. In this case, we noticed that there was similar code in `arc` and `polygon`, so we "factored it out" into `polyline`.

If we had planned ahead, we might have written `polyline` first and avoided refactoring, but often you don't know enough at the beginning of a project to design all the interfaces. Once you start coding, you understand the problem better. Sometimes refactoring is a sign that you have learned something.

A Development Plan

A *development plan* is a process for writing programs. The process we used in this case study is "encapsulation and generalization." The steps of this process are:

1. Start by writing a small program with no function definitions.

2. Once you get the program working, identify a coherent piece of it, encapsulate the piece in a function, and give it a name.

3. Generalize the function by adding appropriate parameters.

4. Repeat steps 1–3 until you have a set of working functions. Copy and paste working code to avoid retyping (and redebugging).

5. Look for opportunities to improve the program by refactoring. For example, if you have similar code in several places, consider factoring it into an appropriately general function.

This process has some drawbacks—we will see alternatives later—but it can be useful if you don't know ahead of time how to divide the program into functions. This approach lets you design as you go along.

Docstring

A *docstring* is a string before a function that explains the interface ("doc" is short for "documentation"). Here is an example:

```
"""
polyline(t, n, len, angle)

Draws n line segments with the given length and
angle (in degrees) between them.  t is a turtle.
"""
function polyline(t, n, len, angle)
    for i in 1:n
        forward(t, len)
        turn(t, -angle)
    end
end
```

Documentation can be accessed in the REPL or in a notebook by typing ? followed by the name of a function or macro, and pressing Enter:

```
help?> polyline
search:

  polyline(t, n, len, angle)

  Draws n line segments with the given length and angle (in degrees) between
  them. t is a turtle.
```

Docstrings are often triple-quoted strings, also known as "multiline" strings because the triple quotes allow the string to span more than one line.

A docstring contains the essential information someone would need to use the function. It explains concisely what the function does (without getting into the details of how it does it). It explains what effect each parameter has on the behavior of the function and what type each parameter should be (if it is not obvious).

Writing this kind of documentation is an important part of interface design. A well-designed interface should be simple to explain; if you have a hard time explaining one of your functions, maybe the interface could be improved.

Debugging

An interface is like a contract between a function and a caller. The caller agrees to provide certain parameters and the function agrees to do certain work.

For example, `polyline` requires four arguments: `t` has to be a turtle; `n` has to be an integer; `len` should be a positive number; and `angle` has to be a number, which is understood to be in degrees.

These requirements are called *preconditions* because they are supposed to be true before the function starts executing. Conversely, conditions at the end of the function are *postconditions*. Postconditions include the intended effect of the function (like drawing line segments) and any side effects (like moving the turtle or making other changes).

Preconditions are the responsibility of the caller. If the caller violates a (properly documented!) precondition and the function doesn't work correctly, the bug is in the caller, not the function.

If the preconditions are satisfied and the postconditions are not, the bug is in the function. If your pre- and postconditions are clear, they can help with debugging.

Glossary

module
: A file that contains a collection of related functions and other definitions.

package
: An external library with additional functionality.

using statement
: A statement that reads a module file and creates a module object.

loop
: A part of a program that can run repeatedly.

encapsulation
: The process of transforming a sequence of statements into a function definition.

generalization
> The process of replacing something unnecessarily specific (like a number) with something appropriately general (like a variable or parameter).

interface
> A description of how to use a function, including the name and descriptions of the arguments and return value.

refactoring
> The process of modifying a working program to improve function interfaces and other qualities of the code.

development plan
> A process for writing programs.

docstring
> A string that appears at the top of a function definition to document the function's interface.

precondition
> A requirement that should be satisfied by the caller before a function starts.

postcondition
> A requirement that should be satisfied by the function before it ends.

Exercises

Exercise 4-8

Enter the code in this chapter in a notebook.

1. Draw a stack diagram that shows the state of the program while executing circle(🐢, radius). You can do the arithmetic by hand or add print statements to the code.

2. The version of arc in "Refactoring" on page 41 is not very accurate because the linear approximation of the circle is always outside the true circle. As a result, the turtle ends up a few pixels away from the correct destination. The solution shown here illustrates a way to reduce the effect of this error. Read the code and see if it makes sense to you. If you draw a diagram, you might see how it works.

```
"""
arc(t, r, angle)

Draws an arc with the given radius and angle:

    t: turtle
    r: radius
```

```
        angle: angle subtended by the arc, in degrees
    """
    function arc(t, r, angle)
        arc_len = 2 * n * r * abs(angle) / 360
        n = trunc(arc_len / 4) + 3
        step_len = arc_len / n
        step_angle = angle / n

        # making a slight left turn before starting reduces
        # the error caused by the linear approximation of the arc
        turn(t, -step_angle/2)
        polyline(t, n, step_len, step_angle)
        turn(t, step_angle/2)
    end
```

Exercise 4-9

Write an appropriately general set of functions that can draw flowers as in Figure 4-2.

Figure 4-2. Turtle flowers

Exercise 4-10

Write an appropriately general set of functions that can draw shapes as in Figure 4-3.

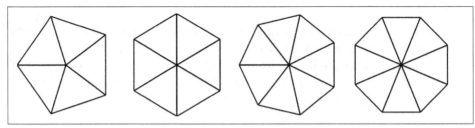

Figure 4-3. Turtle pies

Exercise 4-11

The letters of the alphabet can be constructed from a moderate number of basic elements, like vertical and horizontal lines and a few curves. Design an alphabet that can be drawn with a minimal number of basic elements and then write functions that draw the letters.

You should write one function for each letter, with names draw_a, draw_b, etc., and put your functions in a file named *letters.jl*.

Exercise 4-12

Read about spirals at *https://en.wikipedia.org/wiki/Spiral*; then write a program that draws an Archimedean spiral as in Figure 4-4.

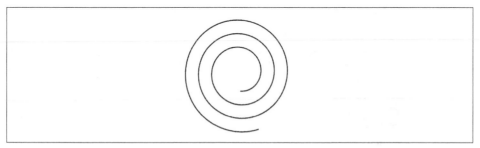

Figure 4-4. Archimedean spiral

CHAPTER 5

Conditionals and Recursion

The main topic of this chapter is the `if` statement, which executes different code depending on the state of the program. But first I want to introduce two new operators: floor division and modulus.

Floor Division and Modulus

The *floor division* operator, ÷ (**\div TAB**), divides two numbers and rounds down to an integer. For example, suppose the running time of a movie is 105 minutes. You might want to know how long that is in hours. Conventional division returns a floating-point number:

```julia
julia> minutes = 105
105
julia> minutes / 60
1.75
```

But we don't normally write hours with decimal points. Floor division returns the integer number of hours, rounding down:

```julia
julia> hours = minutes ÷ 60
1
```

To get the remainder, you could subtract one hour in minutes:

```julia
julia> remainder = minutes - hours * 60
45
```

An alternative is to use the *modulus operator*, %, which divides two numbers and returns the remainder:

```julia
julia> remainder = minutes % 60
45
```

The modulus operator is more useful than it seems. For example, you can check whether one number is divisible by another—if x % y is 0, then x is divisible by y.

Also, you can extract the rightmost digit or digits from a number. For example, x % 10 yields the rightmost digit of an integer x (in base 10). Similarly, x % 100 yields the last two digits.

Boolean Expressions

A *Boolean expression* is an expression that is either true or false. The following examples use the operator ==, which compares two operands and produces true if they are equal and false otherwise:

```
julia> 5 == 5
true
julia> 5 == 6
false
```

true and false are special values that belong to the type Bool; they are not strings:

```
julia> typeof(true)
Bool
julia> typeof(false)
Bool
```

The == operator is one of the *relational operators* (operators that compare their operands). The others are:

```
x != y        # x is not equal to y
x ≠ y         # (\ne TAB)
x > y         # x is greater than y
x < y         # x is less than y
x >= y        # x is greater than or equal to y
x ≥ y         # (\ge TAB)
x <= y        # x is less than or equal to y
x ≤ y         # (\le TAB)
```

Although these operations are probably familiar to you, the Julia symbols are different from the mathematical symbols. A common error is to use a single equals sign (=) instead of a double equals sign (==). Remember that = is an assignment operator and == is a relational operator. There is no such thing as =< or =>.

Logical Operators

There are three *logical operators*: && (and), || (or), and ! (not). The semantics (meaning) of these operators is similar to their meaning in English. For example, x > 0 && x < 10 is true only if x is greater than 0 *and* less than 10.

n % 2 == 0 || n % 3 == 0 is true if *either or both* of the conditions is true; that is, if the number is divisible by 2 *or* 3.

Both && and || associate to the right (i.e., grouped from the right), but && has higher precedence than || does.

Finally, the ! operator negates a Boolean expression, so !(x > y) is true if x > y is false; that is, if x is less than or equal to y.

Conditional Execution

In order to write useful programs, we almost always need the ability to check conditions and change the behavior of the program accordingly. *Conditional statements* give us this ability. The simplest form is the if statement:

```
if x > 0
    println("x is positive")
end
```

The Boolean expression after if is called the *condition*. If it is true, the indented statement runs. If not, nothing happens.

if statements have the same structure as function definitions: a header followed by a body terminated with the keyword end. Statements like this are called *compound statements*.

There is no limit on the number of statements that can appear in the body. Occasionally, it is useful to have a body with no statements (usually as a placeholder for code you haven't written yet):

```
if x < 0
    # TODO: need to handle negative values!
end
```

Alternative Execution

A second form of the if statement is "alternative execution," in which there are two possibilities and the condition determines which one runs. The syntax looks like this:

```
if x % 2 == 0
    println("x is even")
else
```

```
    println("x is odd")
end
```

If the remainder when x is divided by 2 is 0, then we know that x is even, and the program displays an appropriate message. If the condition is false, the second set of statements runs. Since the condition must be true or false, exactly one of the alternatives will run. The alternatives are called *branches*, because they are branches in the flow of execution.

Chained Conditionals

Sometimes there are more than two possibilities and we need more than two branches. One way to express a computation like that is using a *chained conditional*:

```
if x < y
    println("x is less than y")
elseif x > y
    println("x is greater than y")
else
    println("x and y are equal")
end
```

Again, exactly one branch will run. There is no limit on the number of elseif statements. If there is an else clause, it has to be at the end, but there doesn't have to be one:

```
if choice == "a"
    draw_a()
elseif choice == "b"
    draw_b()
elseif choice == "c"
    draw_c()
end
```

Each condition is checked in order. If the first is false, the next is checked, and so on. If one of them is true, the corresponding branch runs and the statement ends. Even if more than one condition is true, only the first true branch runs.

Nested Conditionals

One conditional can also be nested within another. We could have written the example in the previous section like this:

```
if x == y
    println("x and y are equal")
else
    if x < y
        println("x is less than y")
    else
        println("x is greater than y")
```

```
        end
    end
```

The outer conditional contains two branches. The first branch contains a simple statement. The second branch contains another if statement, which has two branches of its own. Those two branches are both simple statements, although they could have been conditional statements as well.

Although the (noncompulsory) indentation of the statements makes the structure apparent, *nested conditionals* become difficult to read very quickly. It is a good idea to avoid them when you can.

Logical operators often provide a way to simplify nested conditional statements. For example, we can rewrite the following code using a single conditional:

```
if 0 < x
    if x < 10
        println("x is a positive single-digit number.")
    end
end
```

The print statement runs only if we make it past both conditionals, so we can get the same effect with the && operator:

```
if 0 < x && x < 10
    println("x is a positive single-digit number.")
end
```

For this kind of condition, Julia provides a more concise syntax:

```
if 0 < x < 10
    println("x is a positive single-digit number.")
end
```

Recursion

It is legal for one function to call another; it is also legal for a function to call itself. It may not be obvious why that is a good thing, but it turns out to be one of the most magical things a program can do. For example, look at the following function:

```
function countdown(n)
    if n ≤ 0
        println("Blastoff!")
    else
        print(n, " ")
        countdown(n-1)
    end
end
```

If n is 0 or negative, it outputs the word "Blastoff!". Otherwise, it outputs n and then calls a function named countdown—itself—passing n-1 as an argument.

What happens if we call this function like this?

```
julia> countdown(3)
3 2 1 Blastoff!
```

The execution of countdown begins with n = 3, and since n is greater than 0, it outputs the value 3, and then calls itself...

The execution of countdown begins with n = 2, and since n is greater than 0, it outputs the value 2, and then calls itself...

The execution of countdown begins with n = 1, and since n is greater than 0, it outputs the value 1, and then calls itself...

The execution of countdown begins with n = 0, and since n is not greater than 0, it outputs the word "Blastoff!" and then returns.

The countdown that got n = 1 returns.

The countdown that got n = 2 returns.

The countdown that got n = 3 returns.

And then you're back in Main.

A function that calls itself is *recursive*; the process of executing it is called *recursion*.

As another example, we can write a function that prints a string n times:

```
function printn(s, n)
    if n ≤ 0
        return
    end
    println(s)
    printn(s, n-1)
end
```

If n <= 0 the *return statement* exits the function. The flow of execution immediately returns to the caller, and the remaining lines of the function don't run.

The rest of the function is similar to countdown: it displays s and then calls itself to display s n-1 additional times. So, the number of lines of output is 1 + (n - 1), which adds up to n.

For simple examples like this, it is probably easier to use a for loop. But we will see examples later that are hard to write with a for loop and easy to write with recursion, so it is good to start early.

Stack Diagrams for Recursive Functions

In "Stack Diagrams" on page 27, we used a stack diagram to represent the state of a program during a function call. The same kind of diagram can help us interpret a recursive function.

Every time a function gets called, Julia creates a frame to contain the function's local variables and parameters. For a recursive function, there might be more than one frame on the stack at the same time.

Figure 5-1 shows a stack diagram for countdown called with n = 3.

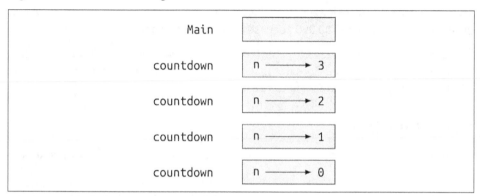

Figure 5-1. Stack diagram

As usual, at the top of the stack is the frame for Main. It is empty because we did not create any variables in Main or pass any arguments to it.

The four countdown frames have different values for the parameter n. The bottom of the stack, where n = 0, is called the *base case*. It does not make a recursive call, so there are no more frames.

Exercise 5-1

As an exercise, draw a stack diagram for printn called with s = "Hello" and n = 2. Then write a function called do_n that takes a function object and a number, n, as arguments, and that calls the given function n times.

Infinite Recursion

If a recursion never reaches a base case, it goes on making recursive calls forever, and the program never terminates. This is known as *infinite recursion*, and it is generally not a good idea. Here is a minimal program with an infinite recursion:

```
function recurse()
    recurse()
end
```

In most programming environments, a program with an infinite recursion does not
really run forever. Julia reports an error message when the maximum recursion depth
is reached:

```
julia> recurse()
ERROR: StackOverflowError:
Stacktrace:
 [1] recurse() at ./REPL[1]:2 (repeats 80000 times)
```

This stacktrace is a little bigger than the one we saw in the previous chapter. When
the error occurs, there are 80,000 recurse frames on the stack!

If you encounter an infinite recursion by accident, review your function to confirm
that there is a base case that does not make a recursive call. And if there is a base case,
check whether you are guaranteed to reach it.

Keyboard Input

The programs we have written so far accept no input from the user. They just do the
same thing every time.

Julia provides a built-in function called readline that stops the program and waits
for the user to type something. When the user presses Return or Enter, the program
resumes and readline returns what the user typed as a string:

```
julia> text = readline()
What are you waiting for?
"What are you waiting for?"
```

Before getting input from the user, it is a good idea to print a prompt telling her what
to type:

```
julia> print("What...is your name? "); readline()
What...is your name? Arthur, King of the Britons!
"Arthur, King of the Britons!"
```

A semicolon (;) allows you to put multiple statements on the same line. In the REPL,
only the last statement returns its value. semicolon (;) allows you to put multiple
statements on the same line. In the REPL, only the last statement returns its value.

If you expect the user to type an integer, you can try to convert the return value to
Int64:

```
julia> println("What...is the airspeed velocity of an unladen swallow?"); speed
= readline()
What...is the airspeed velocity of an unladen swallow?
42
```

```
"42"
julia> parse(Int64, speed)
42
```

But if the user types something other than a string of digits, you get an error:

```
julia> println("What...is the airspeed velocity of an unladen swallow? ");
speed = readline()
What...is the airspeed velocity of an unladen swallow?
What do you mean, an African or a European swallow?
"What do you mean, an African or a European swallow?"
julia> parse(Int64, speed)
ERROR: ArgumentError: invalid base 10 digit 'W' in "What do you mean, an African
  or a European swallow?"
[...]
```

We will see how to handle this kind of error later.

Debugging

When a syntax or runtime error occurs, the error message contains a lot of information. This can be overwhelming. The most useful parts are usually:

- What kind of error it was
- Where it occurred

Syntax errors are usually easy to find, but there are a few gotchas. In general, error messages indicate where the problem was discovered, but the actual error might be earlier in the code, sometimes on a previous line.

The same is true of runtime errors. Suppose you are trying to compute a signal-to-noise ratio in decibels. The formula is:

$$SNR_{db} = 10 \log_{10} \frac{P_{signal}}{P_{noise}}$$

In Julia, you might write something like this:

```
signal_power = 9
noise_power = 10
ratio = signal_power ÷ noise_power
decibels = 10 * log10(ratio)
print(decibels)
```

And you'd get:

```
-Inf
```

This is not the result you expected.

To find the error, it might be useful to print the value of `ratio`, which turns out to be 0. The problem is in line 3, which uses floor division instead of floating-point division.

 You should take the time to read error messages carefully, but don't assume that everything they say is correct.

Glossary

floor division

An operator, denoted ÷, that divides two numbers and rounds down (toward negative infinity) to an integer.

modulus operator

An operator, denoted with a percent sign (%), that works on integers and returns the remainder when one number is divided by another.

Boolean expression

An expression whose value is either `true` or `false`.

relational operator

One of the operators that compares its operands: ==, ≠ (!=), >, <, ≥ (>=), and ≤ (<=).

logical operator

One of the operators that combines Boolean expressions: && (and), || (or), and ! (not).

conditional statement

A statement that controls the flow of execution depending on some condition.

condition

The Boolean expression in a conditional statement that determines which branch runs.

compound statement

A statement that consists of a header and a body. The body is terminated with the keyword end.

branch

One of the alternative sequences of statements in a conditional statement.

chained conditional
> A conditional statement with a series of alternative branches.

nested conditional
> A conditional statement that appears in one of the branches of another conditional statement.

recursive function
> A function that calls itself.

recursion
> The process of calling the function that is currently executing.

return statement
> A statement that causes a function to end immediately and return to the caller.

base case
> A conditional branch in a recursive function that does not make a recursive call.

infinite recursion
> A recursion that doesn't have a base case, or never reaches it. Eventually, an infinite recursion causes a runtime error.

Exercises

Exercise 5-2

The function `time` returns the current Greenwich Mean Time in seconds since "the epoch," which is an arbitrary time used as a reference point. On Unix systems, the epoch is 1 January 1970:

```
julia> time()
1.550846226624217e9
```

Write a script that reads the current time and converts it to a time of day in hours, minutes, and seconds, plus the number of days since the epoch.

Exercise 5-3

Fermat's Last Theorem says that there are no positive integers *a*, *b*, and *c* such that:

$$a^n + b^n = c^n$$

for any value of *n* greater than 2.

1. Write a function named `checkfermat` that takes four parameters—a, b, c, and n— and checks to see if Fermat's theorem holds. If n is greater than 2 and a^n + b^n

== c^n the program should print, "Holy smokes, Fermat was wrong!" Otherwise, the program should print, "No, that doesn't work."

2. Write a function that prompts the user to input values for a, b, c, and n, converts them to integers, and uses checkfermat to check whether they violate Fermat's theorem.

Exercise 5-4

If you are given three sticks, you may or may not be able to arrange them in a triangle. For example, if one of the sticks is 12 inches long and the other two are 1 inch long, you will not be able to get the short sticks to meet in the middle. For any three lengths, there is a simple test to see if it is possible to form a triangle:

> If any of the three lengths is greater than the sum of the other two, then you cannot form a triangle. Otherwise, you can. (If the sum of two lengths equals the third, they form what is called a "degenerate" triangle.)

1. Write a function named istriangle that takes three integers as arguments and prints either "Yes" or "No," depending on whether you can or cannot form a triangle from sticks with the given lengths.

2. Write a function that prompts the user to input three stick lengths, converts them to integers, and uses istriangle to check whether sticks with the given lengths can form a triangle.

Exercise 5-5

What is the output of the following program? Draw a stack diagram that shows the state of the program when it prints the result.

```
function recurse(n, s)
    if n == 0
        println(s)
    else
        recurse(n-1, n+s)
    end
end

recurse(3, 0)
```

1. What would happen if you called this function like this: recurse(-1, 0)?

2. Write a docstring that explains everything someone would need to know in order to use this function (and nothing else).

The following exercises use the ThinkJulia module, described in Chapter 4.

Exercise 5-6

Read the following function and see if you can figure out what it does (see the examples in Chapter 4). Then run it and see if you got it right.

```
function draw(t, length, n)
    if n == 0
        return
    end
    angle = 50
    forward(t, length*n)
    turn(t, -angle)
    draw(t, length, n-1)
    turn(t, 2*angle)
    draw(t, length, n-1)
    turn(t, -angle)
    forward(t, -length*n)
end
```

Exercise 5-7

The Koch curve is a fractal that looks something like Figure 5-2.

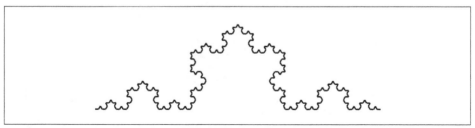

Figure 5-2. A Koch curve

To draw a Koch curve with length x, all you have to do is:

1. Draw a Koch curve with length $\frac{x}{3}$.

2. Turn left 60 degrees.

3. Draw a Koch curve with length $\frac{x}{3}$.

4. Turn right 120 degrees.

5. Draw a Koch curve with length $\frac{x}{3}$.

6. Turn left 60 degrees.

7. Draw a Koch curve with length $\frac{x}{3}$.

The exception is if x is less than 3: in that case, you can just draw a straight line with length x.

1. Write a function called koch that takes a turtle and a length as parameters, and that uses the turtle to draw a Koch curve with the given length.

2. Write a function called snowflake that draws three Koch curves to make the outline of a snowflake.

3. The Koch curve can be generalized in several ways. See *https://en.wikipedia.org/wiki/Koch_snowflake* for examples and implement your favorite.

CHAPTER 6

Fruitful Functions

Many of the Julia functions we have used, such as the math functions, produce return values. But the functions we've written are all void: they have an effect, like printing a value or moving a turtle, but they return nothing. In this chapter you will learn to write fruitful functions.

Return Values

Calling a function generates a return value, which we usually assign to a variable or use as part of an expression:

```
e = exp(1.0)
height = radius * sin(radians)
```

The functions we have written so far are void. Speaking casually, they have no return value; more precisely, their return value is nothing. In this chapter, we are (finally) going to write fruitful functions. The first example is area, which returns the area of a circle with the given radius:

```
function area(radius)
    a = π * radius^2
    return a
end
```

We have seen the return statement before, but in a fruitful function the return statement includes an expression. This statement means: "Return immediately from this function and use the following expression as a return value." The expression can be arbitrarily complicated, so we could have written this function more concisely:

```
function area(radius)
    π * radius^2
end
```

However, *temporary variables* like a and explicit return statements can make debugging easier.

The value returned by a function is the value of the last expression evaluated, which, by default, is the last expression in the body of the function definition.

Sometimes it is useful to have multiple return statements, one in each branch of a conditional:

```
function absvalue(x)
    if x < 0
        return -x
    else
        return x
    end
end
```

Since these return statements are in an alternative conditional, only one runs.

As soon as a return statement runs, the function terminates without executing any subsequent statements. Code that appears after a return statement, or any other place the flow of execution can never reach, is called *dead code*.

In a fruitful function, it is a good idea to ensure that every possible path through the program hits a return statement. Consider this example:

```
function absvalue(x)
    if x < 0
        return -x
    end
    if x > 0
        return x
    end
end
```

This function is incorrect because if x happens to be 0, neither condition is true, and the function ends without hitting a return statement. If the flow of execution gets to the end of a function, the return value is nothing, which is not the absolute value of 0.

```
julia> show(absvalue(0))
nothing
```

 Julia provides a built-in function called abs that computes absolute values.

Exercise 6-1

Write a `compare` function that takes two values, x and y, and returns 1 if x > y, 0 if x == y, and -1 if x < y.

Incremental Development

As you write larger functions, you might find yourself spending more time debugging.

To deal with increasingly complex programs, you might want to try a process called *incremental development*. The goal of incremental development is to avoid long debugging sessions by adding and testing only a small amount of code at a time.

As an example, suppose you want to find the distance between two points, given by the coordinates (x_1, y_1) and (x_2, y_2). By the Pythagorean theorem, the distance is:

$$d = \sqrt{(x_2 - x_1)^2 + (y_2 - y_1)^2}$$

The first step is to consider what a distance function should look like in Julia. In other words, what are the inputs (parameters) and what is the output (return value)?

In this case, the inputs are two points, which you can represent using four numbers. The return value is the distance represented by a floating-point value.

Immediately you can write an outline of the function:

```
function distance(x₁, y₁, x₂, y₂)
    0.0
end
```

Obviously, this version doesn't compute distances; it always returns zero. But it is syntactically correct, and it runs, which means that you can test it before you make it more complicated. The subscript numbers are available in the Unicode character encoding (**_1 TAB**, **_2 TAB**, etc.).

To test the new function, call it with sample arguments:

```
distance(1, 2, 4, 6)
```

I chose these values so that the horizontal distance is 3 and the vertical distance is 4; that way, the result is 5, the hypotenuse of a 3-4-5 triangle. When testing a function, it is useful to know the right answer.

At this point we have confirmed that the function is syntactically correct, and we can start adding code to the body. A reasonable next step is to find the differences $x_2 - x_1$ and $y_2 - y_1$. The next version stores those values in temporary variables and prints them with the @show macro:

```
function distance(x₁, y₁, x₂, y₂)
    dx = x₂ - x₁
    dy = y₂ - y₁
    @show dx dy
    0.0
end
```

If the function is working, it should display dx = 3 and dy = 4. If so, we know that the function is getting the right arguments and performing the first computation correctly. If not, there are only a few lines to check.

Next, we compute the sum of squares of dx and dy:

```
function distance(x₁, y₁, x₂, y₂)
    dx = x₂ - x₁
    dy = y₂ - y₁
    d² = dx^2 + dy^2
    @show d²
    0.0
end
```

Again, you would run the program at this stage and check the output (which should be 25). Superscript numbers are also available (**\^2 TAB**). Finally, you can use sqrt to compute and return the result:

```
function distance(x₁, y₁, x₂, y₂)
    dx = x₂ - x₁
    dy = y₂ - y₁
    d² = dx^2 + dy^2
    sqrt(d²)
end
```

If that works correctly, you are done. Otherwise, you might want to print the value of sqrt(d²) before the return statement.

The final version of the function doesn't display anything when it runs; it only returns a value. The print statements we wrote are useful for debugging, but once you get the function working, you should remove them. Code like that is called *scaffolding* because it is helpful for building the program but is not part of the final product.

When you start out, you should add only a line or two of code at a time. As you gain more experience, you might find yourself writing and debugging bigger chunks. Either way, incremental development can save you a lot of debugging time.

The key aspects of the process are:

1. Start with a working program and make small, incremental changes. At any point, if there is an error, you should have a good idea where it is.

2. Use variables to hold intermediate values so you can display and check them.

3. Once the program is working, you might want to remove some of the scaffolding or consolidate multiple statements into compound expressions, but only if it does not make the program difficult to read.

Exercise 6-2

Use incremental development to write a function called hypotenuse that returns the length of the hypotenuse of a right triangle given the lengths of the other two legs as arguments. Record each stage of the development process as you go.

Composition

As you should expect by now, you can call one function from within another. As an example, we'll write a function that takes two points, the center of the circle and a point on the perimeter, and computes the area of the circle.

Assume that the center point is stored in the variables xc and yc, and the perimeter point is in xp and yp. The first step is to find the radius of the circle, which is the distance between the two points. We just wrote a function, distance, that does that:

```
radius = distance(xc, yc, xp, yp)
```

The next step is to find the area of a circle with that radius; we just wrote that, too:

```
result = area(radius)
```

Encapsulating these steps in a function, we get:

```
function circlearea(xc, yc, xp, yp)
    radius = distance(xc, yc, xp, yp)
    result = area(radius)
    return result
end
```

The temporary variables radius and result are useful for development and debugging, but once the program is working, we can make it more concise by composing the function calls:

```
function circlearea(xc, yc, xp, yp)
    area(distance(xc, yc, xp, yp))
end
```

Boolean Functions

Functions can return Booleans, which is often convenient for hiding complicated tests inside functions. For example:

```
function isdivisible(x, y)
    if x % y == 0
```

```
        return true
    else
        return false
    end
end
```

It is common to give Boolean functions names that sound like yes/no questions; `isdivisible` returns either `true` or `false` to indicate whether x is divisible by y.

Here is an example:

```
julia> isdivisible(6, 4)
false
julia> isdivisible(6, 3)
true
```

The result of the == operator is a Boolean, so we can write the function more concisely by returning it directly:

```
function isdivisible(x, y)
    x % y == 0
end
```

Boolean functions are often used in conditional statements:

```
if isdivisible(x, y)
    println("x is divisible by y")
end
```

It might be tempting to write something like:

```
if isdivisible(x, y) == true
    println("x is divisible by y")
end
```

But the extra comparison with `true` is unnecessary.

Exercise 6-3

Write a function `isbetween(x, y, z)` that returns `true` if x ≤ y ≤ z or `false` otherwise.

More Recursion

We have only covered a small subset of Julia, but you might be interested to know that this subset is a *complete* programming language, which means that anything that can be computed can be expressed in this language. Any program ever written could be rewritten using only the language features you have learned so far (actually, you would need a few commands to control devices like the mouse, disks, etc., but that's all).

Proving that claim is a nontrivial exercise first accomplished by Alan Turing, one of the first computer scientists (some would argue that he was a mathematician, but a lot of early computer scientists started as mathematicians). Accordingly, it is known as the Turing thesis. For a more complete (and accurate) discussion of the Turing thesis, I recommend Michael Sipser's book *Introduction to the Theory of Computation* (Cengage).

To give you an idea of what you can do with the tools you have learned so far, we'll evaluate a few recursively defined mathematical functions. A recursive definition is similar to a circular definition, in the sense that the definition contains a reference to the thing being defined. A truly circular definition is not very useful:

vorpal
    An adjective used to describe something that is vorpal.

If you saw that definition in the dictionary, you might be annoyed. On the other hand, if you looked up the definition of the factorial function, denoted with the symbol !, you might get something like this:

$$n! = \begin{cases} 1 & \text{if } n = 0 \\ n(n-1)! & \text{if } n > 0 \end{cases}$$

This definition says that the factorial of 0 is 1, and the factorial of any other value, n, is n multiplied by the factorial of $n - 1$.

So, 3! is 3 times 2!, which is 2 times 1!, which is 1 times 0!. Putting it all together, 3! equals 3 times 2 times 1 times 1, which is 6.

If you can write a recursive definition of something, you can write a Julia program to evaluate it. The first step is to decide what the parameters should be. In this case it should be clear that factorial takes an integer:

```
function fact(n) end
```

If the argument happens to be 0, all we have to do is return 1:

```
function fact(n)
    if n == 0
        return 1
    end
end
```

Otherwise, and this is the interesting part, we have to make a recursive call to find the factorial of n-1 and then multiply it by n:

```
function fact(n)
    if n == 0
        return 1
    else
```

```
            recurse = fact(n-1)
            result = n * recurse
            return result
        end
    end
```

The flow of execution for this program is similar to the flow of countdown in "Recursion" on page 53. If we call fact with the value 3:

Since 3 is not 0, we take the second branch and calculate the factorial of n-1...

Since 2 is not 0, we take the second branch and calculate the factorial of n-1...

Since 1 is not 0, we take the second branch and calculate the factorial of n-1...

Since 0 equals 0, we take the first branch and return 1 without making any more recursive calls.

The return value, 1, is multiplied by n, which is 1, and the result is returned.

The return value, 1, is multiplied by n, which is 2, and the result is returned.

The return value 2 is multiplied by n, which is 3, and the result, 6, becomes the return value of the function call that started the whole process.

Figure 6-1 shows what the stack diagram looks like for this sequence of function calls.

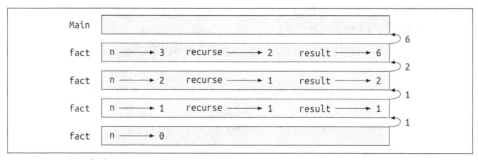

Figure 6-1. Stack diagram

The return values are shown being passed back up the stack. In each frame, the return value is the value of result, which is the product of n and recurse.

In the last frame, the local variables recurse and result do not exist, because the branch that creates them does not run.

 Julia provides the function factorial to calculate the factorial of an integer number.

Leap of Faith

Following the flow of execution is one way to read programs, but it can quickly become overwhelming. An alternative is what I call the "leap of faith." When you come to a function call, instead of following the flow of execution, you *assume* that the function works correctly and returns the right result.

In fact, you are already practicing this leap of faith when you use built-in functions. When you call cos or exp, you don't examine the bodies of those functions. You just assume that they work because the people who wrote the built-in functions were good programmers.

The same is true when you call one of your own functions. For example, in "Boolean Functions" on page 67, we wrote a function called isdivisible that determines whether one number is divisible by another. Once we have convinced ourselves that this function is correct—by examining the code and testing it—we can use the function without looking at the body again.

The same is true of recursive programs. In our example, when you get to the recursive call, instead of following the flow of execution, you should assume that the recursive call works (returns the correct result) and then ask yourself, "Assuming that I can find the factorial of n-1, can I compute the factorial of n?" It is clear that you can, by multiplying by n.

Of course, it's a bit strange to assume that the function works correctly when you haven't finished writing it, but that's why it's called a leap of faith!

One More Example

After factorial, the most common example of a recursively defined mathematical function is Fibonacci (*http://bit.ly/2OQ2uQq*):

$$fib(n) = \begin{cases} 0 & \text{if } n = 0 \\ 1 & \text{if } n = 1 \\ fib(n-1) + fib(n-2) & \text{if } n > 1 \end{cases}$$

Translated into Julia, it looks like this:

```
function fib(n)
    if n == 0
        return 0
    elseif n == 1
        return 1
    else
        return fib(n-1) + fib(n-2)
```

```
        end
    end
```

If you try to follow the flow of execution here, even for fairly small values of n, your head explodes. But if you take the leap of faith and you assume that the two recursive calls work correctly, then it is clear that you get the right result by adding them together.

Checking Types

What happens if we call `fact` and give it `1.5` as an argument?

```
julia> fact(1.5)
ERROR: StackOverflowError:
Stacktrace:
 [1] fact(::Float64) at ./REPL[3]:2
```

It looks like an infinite recursion. How can that be? The function has a base case—when n `==` `0`. But if n is not an integer, we can *miss* the base case and recurse forever.

In the first recursive call, the value of n is `0.5`. In the next, it is `-0.5`. From there, it gets smaller (more negative), but it will never be `0`.

We have two choices. We can try to generalize the factorial function to work with floating-point numbers, or we can make `fact` check the type of its argument. The first option is called the gamma function, and it's a little beyond the scope of this book. So we'll go for the second.

We can use the built-in operator `isa` to verify the type of the argument. While we're at it, we can also make sure the argument is positive:

```
function fact(n)
    if !(n isa Int64)
        error("Factorial is only defined for integers.")
    elseif n < 0
        error("Factorial is not defined for negative integers.")
    elseif n == 0
        return 1
    else
        return n * fact(n-1)
    end
end
```

The first base case handles nonintegers; the second handles negative integers. In both cases, the program prints an error message and returns `nothing` to indicate that something went wrong:

```
julia> fact("fred")
ERROR: Factorial is only defined for integers.
julia> fact(-2)
ERROR: Factorial is not defined for negative integers.
```

If we get past both checks, we know that n is positive or 0, so we can prove that the recursion terminates.

This program demonstrates a pattern sometimes called a *guardian*. The first two conditionals act as guardians, protecting the code that follows from values that might cause an error. The guardians make it possible to prove the correctness of the code.

In "Catching Exceptions" on page 170 we will see a more flexible alternative to printing an error message: raising an exception.

Debugging

Breaking a large program into smaller functions creates natural checkpoints for debugging. If a function is not working, there are three possibilities to consider:

- There is something wrong with the arguments the function is getting; a precondition is violated.
- There is something wrong with the function; a postcondition is violated.
- There is something wrong with the return value or the way it is being used.

To rule out the first possibility, you can add a print statement at the beginning of the function and display the values of the parameters (and maybe their types). Or you can write code that checks the preconditions explicitly.

If the parameters look good, add a print statement before each return statement and display the return value. If possible, check the result by hand. Consider calling the function with values that make it easy to check the result (as in "Incremental Development" on page 65).

If the function seems to be working, look at the function call to make sure the return value is being used correctly (or used at all!).

Adding print statements at the beginning and end of a function can help make the flow of execution more visible. For example, here is a version of fact with print statements:

```
function fact(n)
    space = " " ^ (4 * n)
    println(space, "factorial ", n)
    if n == 0
        println(space, "returning 1")
        return 1
    else
        recurse = fact(n-1)
        result = n * recurse
        println(space, "returning ", result)
        return result
```

```
        end
    end
```

`space` is a string of space characters that controls the indentation of the output:

```
julia> fact(4)
                factorial 4
            factorial 3
        factorial 2
    factorial 1
factorial 0
returning 1
    returning 1
        returning 2
            returning 6
                returning 24
24
```

If you are confused about the flow of execution, this kind of output can be helpful. It takes some time to develop effective scaffolding, but a little bit of scaffolding can save a lot of debugging.

Glossary

temporary variable
    A variable used to store an intermediate value in a complex calculation.

dead code
    Part of a program that can never run, often because it appears after a `return` statement.

incremental development
    A program development plan intended to avoid debugging by adding and testing only a small amount of code at a time.

scaffolding
    Code that is used during program development but is not part of the final version.

guardian
    A programming pattern that uses a conditional statement to check for and handle circumstances that might cause an error.

Exercises

Exercise 6-4

Draw a stack diagram for the following program. What does the program print?

```
function b(z)
    prod = a(z, z)
    println(z, " ", prod)
    prod
end

function a(x, y)
    x = x + 1
    x * y
end

function c(x, y, z)
    total = x + y + z
    square = b(total)^2
    square
end

x = 1
y = x + 1
println(c(x, y+3, x+y))
```

Exercise 6-5

The Ackermann function (*http://bit.ly/2TW2T4X*), $A(m, n)$, is defined as:

$$A(m, n) = \begin{cases} n + 1 & \text{if } m = 0 \\ A(m - 1, 1) & \text{if } m > 0 \text{ and } n = 0 \\ A(m - 1, A(m, n - 1)) & \text{if } m > 0 \text{ and } n > 0 \end{cases}$$

Write a function named ack that evaluates the Ackermann function. Use your function to evaluate ack(3, 4), which should be 125. What happens for larger values of m and n?

Exercise 6-6

A palindrome is a word that is spelled the same backward and forward, like "noon" or "redivider." Recursively, a word is a palindrome if the first and last letters are the same and the middle is a palindrome.

The following are functions that take a string argument and return the first, last, and middle letters:

```
function first(word)
    first = firstindex(word)
    word[first]
end

function last(word)
    last = lastindex(word)
```

```
        word[last]
    end

    function middle(word)
        first = firstindex(word)
        last = lastindex(word)
        word[nextind(word, first) : prevind(word, last)]
    end
```

We'll see how they work in Chapter 8.

1. Test these functions out. What happens if you call middle with a string with two letters? One letter? What about the empty string, which is written "" and contains no letters?

2. Write a function called ispalindrome that takes a string argument and returns true if it is a palindrome and false otherwise. Remember that you can use the built-in function length to check the length of a string.

Exercise 6-7

A number, a, is a power of b if it is divisible by b and $\frac{a}{b}$ is a power of b. Write a function called ispower that takes parameters a and b and returns true if a is a power of b.

 You will have to think about the base case.

Exercise 6-8

The greatest common divisor (GCD) of a and b is the largest number that divides both of them with no remainder.

One way to find the GCD of two numbers is based on the observation that if r is the remainder when a is divided by b, then gcd(a, b) = gcd(b, r). As a base case, we can use gcd(a, 0) = a.

Write a function called gcd that takes parameters a and b and returns their greatest common divisor.

Credit: This exercise is based on an example from Hal Abelson and Gerald Jay Sussman's *Structure and Interpretation of Computer Programs* (MIT Press).

CHAPTER 7

Iteration

This chapter is about iteration, which is the ability to run a block of statements repeatedly. We saw a kind of iteration, using recursion, in "Recursion" on page 53. We saw another kind, using a for loop, in "Simple Repetition" on page 36. In this chapter we'll see yet another kind, using a while statement. But first I want to say a little more about variable assignment.

Reassignment

As you may have discovered, it is legal to make more than one assignment to the same variable. A new assignment makes an existing variable refer to a new value (and stop referring to the old value):

```
julia> x = 5
5
julia> x = 7
7
```

The first time we display x, its value is 5; the second time, its value is 7.

Figure 7-1 shows what *reassignment* looks like in a state diagram.

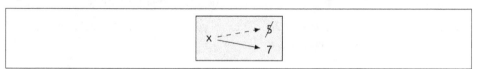

Figure 7-1. State diagram

At this point I want to address a common source of confusion. Because Julia uses the equals sign (=) for assignment, it is tempting to interpret a statement like a = b as a mathematical proposition of equality; that is, the claim that a and b are equal. But this interpretation is wrong.

First, equality is a symmetric relationship and assignment is not. For example, in mathematics, if $a = 7$ then $7 = a$. But in Julia, the statement a = 7 is legal and 7 = a is not.

Also, in mathematics, a proposition of equality is either true or false for all time. If $a = b$ now, then a will always equal b. In Julia, an assignment statement can make two variables equal, but they don't have to stay that way:

```
julia> a = 5
5
julia> b = a      # a and b are now equal
5
julia> a = 3      # a and b are no longer equal
3
julia> b
5
```

The third line changes the value of a but does not change the value of b, so they are no longer equal.

Reassigning variables is often useful, but you should use it with caution. If the values of variables change frequently, it can make the code difficult to read and debug.

It is illegal to define a function that has the same name as a previously defined variable.

Updating Variables

A common kind of reassignment is an *update*, where the new value of the variable depends on the old:

```
julia> x = x + 1
8
```

This means "get the current value of x, add 1, and then update x with the new value."

If you try to update a variable that doesn't exist, you get an error, because Julia evaluates the right side before it assigns a value to x:

```
julia> y = y + 1
ERROR: UndefVarError: y not defined
```

Before you can update a variable, you have to *initialize* it, usually with a simple assignment:

```
julia> y = 0
0
```

```
julia> y = y + 1
1
```

Updating a variable by adding 1 is called an *increment*; subtracting 1 is called a *decrement*.

The while Statement

Computers are often used to automate repetitive tasks. Repeating identical or similar tasks without making errors is something that computers do well and people do poorly. In a computer program, repetition is also called *iteration*.

We have already seen two functions, countdown and printn, that iterate using recursion. Because iteration is so common, Julia provides language features to make it easier. One is the for statement we saw in "Simple Repetition" on page 36. We'll get back to that later.

Another is the *while statement*. Here is a version of countdown that uses a while statement:

```
function countdown(n)
    while n > 0
        print(n, " ")
        n = n - 1
    end
    println("Blastoff!")
end
```

You can almost read the while statement as if it were English. It means, "While n is greater than 0, display the value of n and then decrement n. When you get to 0, display the word "Blastoff!""

More formally, here is the flow of execution for a while statement:

1. Determine whether the condition is true or false.

2. If false, exit the while statement and continue execution at the next statement.

3. If the condition is true, run the body and then go back to step 1.

This type of flow is called a loop because the third step loops back around to the top.

The body of the loop should change the value of one or more variables so that the condition becomes false eventually and the loop terminates. Otherwise, the loop will repeat forever, which is called an *infinite loop*. An endless source of amusement for computer scientists is the observation that the directions on shampoo bottles, "Lather, rinse, repeat," are an infinite loop.

In the case of countdown, we can prove that the loop terminates: if n is 0 or negative, the loop never runs. Otherwise, n gets smaller each time through the loop, so eventually we have to get to 0.

For some other loops, it is not so easy to tell. For example:

```
function seq(n)
    while n != 1
        println(n)
        if n % 2 == 0          # n is even
            n = n / 2
        else                   # n is odd
            n = n*3 + 1
        end
    end
end
```

The condition for this loop is n != 1, so the loop will continue until n is 1, which makes the condition false.

Each time through the loop, the program outputs the value of n and then checks whether it is even or odd. If it is even, n is divided by 2. If it is odd, the value of n is replaced with n*3 + 1. For example, if the argument passed to seq is 3, the resulting values of n are 3, 10, 5, 16, 8, 4, 2, 1.

Since n sometimes increases and sometimes decreases, there is no obvious proof that n will ever reach 1, or that the program terminates. For some particular values of n, we can prove termination. For example, if the starting value is a power of two, n will be even every time through the loop until it reaches 1. The previous example ends with such a sequence, starting with 16.

The hard question is whether we can prove that this program terminates for all positive values of n. So far, no one has been able to prove it or disprove it! (*http://bit.ly/2KkdE1B*)

Exercise 7-1

Rewrite the function printn from "Recursion" on page 53 using iteration instead of recursion.

break

Sometimes you don't know it's time to end a loop until you get halfway through the body. In that case you can use the *break statement* to jump out of the loop.

For example, suppose you want to take input from the user until they type **done**. You could write:

```
while true
    print("> ")
    line = readline()
    if line == "done"
        break
    end
    println(line)
end
println("Done!")
```

The loop condition is true, which is always true, so the loop runs until it hits the break statement.

Each time through, it prompts the user with an angle bracket. If the user types **done**, the break statement exits the loop. Otherwise, the program echoes whatever the user types and goes back to the top of the loop. Here's a sample run:

```
> not done
not done
> done
Done!
```

This way of writing while loops is common because you can check the condition anywhere in the loop (not just at the top) and you can express the stop condition affirmatively ("stop when this happens") rather than negatively ("keep going until that happens").

continue

The break statement exits the loop. When a continue statement is encountered inside a loop, control jumps to the beginning of the loop for the next iteration, skipping the execution of statements inside the body of the loop for the current iteration. For example, this

```
for i in 1:10
    if i % 3 == 0
        continue
    end
    print(i, " ")
end
```

outputs

```
1 2 4 5 7 8 10
```

If i is divisible by 3, the continue statement stops the current iteration and the next iteration starts. Only the numbers in the range 1 to 10 not divisible by 3 are printed.

Square Roots

Loops are often used in programs that compute numerical results by starting with an approximate answer and iteratively improving it.

For example, one way of computing square roots is Newton's method. Suppose that you want to know the square root of a. If you start with almost any estimate, x, you can compute a better estimate with the following formula:

$$y = \frac{1}{2}\left(x + \frac{a}{x}\right)$$

For example, if a is 4 and x is 3:

```
julia> a = 4
4
julia> x = 3
3
julia> y = (x + a/x) / 2
2.1666666666666665
```

The result is closer to the correct answer ($\sqrt{4} = 2$). If we repeat the process with the new estimate, it gets even closer:

```
julia> x = y
2.1666666666666665
julia> y = (x + a/x) / 2
2.0064102564102564
```

After a few more updates, the estimate is almost exact:

```
julia> x = y
2.0064102564102564
julia> y = (x + a/x) / 2
2.0000102400262145
julia> x = y
2.0000102400262145
julia> y = (x + a/x) / 2
2.0000000000262146
```

In general we don't know ahead of time how many steps it takes to get to the right answer, but we know when we get there because the estimate stops changing:

```
julia> x = y
2.0000000000262146
julia> y = (x + a/x) / 2
2.0
julia> x = y
2.0
julia> y = (x + a/x) / 2
2.0
```

When y == x, we can stop. Here is a loop that starts with an initial estimate, x, and improves it until it stops changing:

```
while true
    println(x)
    y = (x + a/x) / 2
    if y == x
        break
    end
    x = y
end
```

For most values of a this works fine, but in general it is dangerous to test float equality. Floating-point values are only approximately right: most rational numbers, like $\frac{1}{3}$, and irrational numbers, like $\sqrt{2}$, can't be represented exactly with a Float64.

Rather than checking whether x and y are exactly equal, it is safer to use the built-in function abs to compute the absolute value, or magnitude, of the difference between them:

```
if abs(y-x) < ε
    break
end
```

where ε (**\varepsilon TAB**) has a value like 0.0000001 that determines how close is close enough.

Algorithms

Newton's method is an example of an *algorithm*: it is a mechanical process for solving a category of problems (in this case, computing square roots).

To understand what an algorithm is, it might help to start with something that is not an algorithm. When you learned to multiply single-digit numbers, you probably memorized the multiplication table. In effect, you memorized 100 specific solutions. That kind of knowledge is not algorithmic.

But if you were "lazy," you might have learned a few tricks. For example, to find the product of n and 9, you can write $n - 1$ as the first digit and $10 - n$ as the second digit. This trick is a general solution for multiplying any single-digit number by 9. That's an algorithm!

Similarly, the techniques you learned for addition with carrying, subtraction with borrowing, and long division are all algorithms. One of the characteristics of algorithms is that they do not require any intelligence to carry out. They are mechanical processes where each step follows from the last according to a simple set of rules.

Executing algorithms is boring, but designing them is interesting, intellectually challenging, and a central part of computer science.

Some of the things that people do naturally, without difficulty or conscious thought, are the hardest to express algorithmically. Understanding natural language is a good example. We all do it, but so far no one has been able to explain *how* we do it, at least not in the form of an algorithm.

Debugging

As you start writing bigger programs, you might find yourself spending more time debugging. More code means more chances to make an error and more places for bugs to hide.

One way to cut your debugging time is "debugging by bisection." For example, if there are 100 lines in your program and you check them one at a time, it will take 100 steps.

Instead, try to break the problem in half. Look at the middle of the program, or near it, for an intermediate value you can check. Add a print statement (or something else that has a verifiable effect) and run the program.

If the midpoint check is incorrect, there must be a problem in the first half of the program. If it is correct, the problem is in the second half.

Every time you perform a check like this, you halve the number of lines you have to search. In theory, after six steps (which is significantly fewer than 100), you'll be down to one or two lines of code.

In practice, it is not always clear what the "middle of the program" is and not always possible to check it. It doesn't make sense to count lines and find the exact midpoint. Instead, think about places in the program where there might be errors and places where it is easy to put a check. Then choose a spot where you think the chances are about the same that the bug is before or after the check.

Glossary

reassignment
> Assigning a new value to a variable that already exists.

update
> An assignment where the new value of the variable depends on the old.

initialization
> An assignment that gives an initial value to a variable that will be updated.

increment
> An update that increases the value of a variable (often by 1).

decrement

An update that decreases the value of a variable.

iteration

Repeated execution of a set of statements using either a recursive function call or a loop.

while *statement*

A statement that allows iterations controlled by a condition.

infinite loop

A loop in which the terminating condition is never satisfied.

break *statement*

A statement allowing you to jump out of a loop.

continue *statement*

A statement inside a loop that jumps to the beginning of the loop for the next iteration.

algorithm

A general process for solving a category of problems.

Exercises

Exercise 7-2

Copy the loop from "Square Roots" on page 82 and encapsulate it in a function called mysqrt that takes a as a parameter, chooses a reasonable value of x, and returns an estimate of the square root of a.

To test it, write a function named testsquareroot that prints a table like this:

```
a    mysqrt               sqrt                 diff
-    ------               ----                 ----
1.0  1.0                  1.0                  0.0
2.0  1.414213562373095    1.4142135623730951   2.220446049250313e-16
3.0  1.7320508075688772   1.7320508075688772   0.0
4.0  2.0                  2.0                  0.0
5.0  2.23606797749979     2.23606797749979     0.0
6.0  2.449489742783178    2.449489742783178    0.0
7.0  2.6457513110645907   2.6457513110645907   0.0
8.0  2.82842712474619     2.8284271247461903   4.440892098500626e-16
9.0  3.0                  3.0                  0.0
```

The first column is a number, a; the second column is the square root of a computed with mysqrt; the third column is the square root computed by sqrt; and the fourth column is the absolute value of the difference between the two estimates.

Exercise 7-3

The built-in function `Meta.parse` takes a string and transforms it into an expression. This expression can be evaluated in Julia with the function `Core.eval`. For example:

```
julia> expr = Meta.parse("1+2*3")
:(1 + 2 * 3)
julia> eval(expr)
7
julia> expr = Meta.parse("sqrt(n)")
:(sqrt(n))
julia> eval(expr)
1.7724538509055159
```

Write a function called `evalloop` that iteratively prompts the user, takes the resulting input and evaluates it using `eval`, and prints the result. It should continue until the user enters **done**, and then return the value of the last expression it evaluated.

Exercise 7-4

The mathematician Srinivasa Ramanujan found an infinite series that can be used to generate a numerical approximation of $\frac{1}{\pi}$:

$$\frac{1}{\pi} = \frac{2\sqrt{2}}{9801} \sum_{k=0}^{\infty} \frac{(4k)!(1103 + 26390k)}{(k!)^4 396^{4k}}$$

Write a function called `estimatepi` that uses this formula to compute and return an estimate of π. It should use a `while` loop to compute terms of the summation until the last term is smaller than `1e-15` (which is Julia notation for 10^{-15}). You can check the result by comparing it to π.

CHAPTER 8

Strings

Strings are not like integers, floats, and Booleans. A string is a *sequence*, which means it is an ordered collection of other values. In this chapter you'll see how to access the characters that make up a string, and you'll learn about some of the string helper functions provided by Julia.

Characters

English language speakers are familiar with characters such as the letters of the alphabet (A, B, C, …), numerals, and common punctuation. These characters are standardized and mapped to integer values between 0 and 127 by the *ASCII standard* (American Standard Code for Information Interchange).

There are, of course, many other characters used in non-English languages, including variants of the ASCII characters with accents and other modifications, related scripts such as Cyrillic and Greek, and scripts completely unrelated to ASCII and English, including Arabic, Chinese, Hebrew, Hindi, Japanese, and Korean.

The *Unicode standard* tackles the complexities of what exactly a character is, and is generally accepted as the definitive standard addressing this problem. It provides a unique number for every character on a worldwide scale.

A Char value represents a single character and is surrounded by single quotes:

```
julia> 'x'
'x': ASCII/Unicode U+0078 (category Ll: Letter, lowercase)
julia> '🍌'
'🍌': Unicode U+01f34c (category So: Symbol, other)
julia> typeof('x')
Char
```

Even emojis are part of the Unicode standard (**\:banana: TAB**).

A String Is a Sequence

A string is a sequence of characters. You can access the characters one at a time with the bracket operator ([ ]):

```
julia> fruit = "banana"
"banana"
julia> letter = fruit[1]
'b': ASCII/Unicode U+0062 (category Ll: Letter, lowercase)
```

The second statement selects character number 1 from `fruit` and assigns it to `letter`.

The expression in brackets is called an *index*. The index indicates which character in the sequence you want (hence the name).

All indexing in Julia is 1-based—the first element of any integer-indexed object is found at index 1 and the last element at index end:

```
julia> fruit[end]
'a': ASCII/Unicode U+0061 (category Ll: Letter, lowercase)
```

As an index, you can use an expression that contains variables and operators:

```
julia> i = 1
1
julia> fruit[i+1]
'a': ASCII/Unicode U+0061 (category Ll: Letter, lowercase)
julia> fruit[end-1]
'n': ASCII/Unicode U+006e (category Ll: Letter, lowercase)
```

But the value of the index has to be an integer. Otherwise, you get:

```
julia> letter = fruit[1.5]
ERROR: MethodError: no method matching getindex(::String, ::Float64)
```

length

`length` is a built-in function that returns the number of characters in a string:

```
julia> fruits = "🍎 🍏 🍐"
"🍎 🍏 🍐"
julia> len = length(fruits)
5
```

To get the last letter of a string, you might be tempted to try something like this:

```
julia> last = fruits[len]
' ': ASCII/Unicode U+0020 (category Zs: Separator, space)
```

But you might not get what you expect.

Strings are encoded using *UTF-8 encoding*. UTF-8 is a variable-width encoding, meaning that not all characters are encoded in the same number of bytes.

The function `sizeof` gives the number of bytes in a string:

```
julia> sizeof("🍎")
4
```

Because an emoji is encoded in 4 bytes and string indexing is byte-based, the fifth element of `fruits` is a SPACE.

This also means that not every byte index into a UTF-8 string is necessarily a valid index for a character. If you index into a string at an invalid byte index, an error is thrown:

```
julia> fruits[2]
ERROR: StringIndexError("🍎 🍊 🍐", 2)
```

In the case of `fruits`, the character 🍎 is a 4-byte character, so the indices 2, 3, and 4 are invalid and the next character's index is 5; this next valid index can be computed by `nextind(fruits, 1)`, the next index after that by `nextind(fruits, 5)` and so on.

Traversal

A lot of computations involve processing a string one character at a time. Often they start at the beginning, select each character in turn, do something to it, and continue until the end. This pattern of processing is called a *traversal*. One way to write a traversal is with a `while` loop:

```
index = firstindex(fruits)
while index <= sizeof(fruits)
    letter = fruits[index]
    println(letter)
    global index = nextind(fruits, index)
end
```

This loop traverses the string and displays each letter on a line by itself. The loop condition is `index <= sizeof(fruit)`, so when `index` is larger than the number of bytes in the string, the condition is `false` and the body of the loop doesn't run.

The function `firstindex` returns the first valid byte index. The keyword `global` before `index` indicates that we want to reassign the variable `index` defined in `Main` (see "Global Variables" on page 135).

Exercise 8-1

Write a function that takes a string as an argument and displays the letters backward, one per line.

Another way to write a traversal is with a `for` loop:

```
for letter in fruits
    println(letter)
end
```

Each time through the loop, the next character in the string is assigned to the variable `letter`. The loop continues until no characters are left.

The following example shows how to use concatenation (string multiplication) and a for loop to generate an abecedarian series (i.e., in alphabetical order). In Robert McCloskey's book *Make Way for Ducklings* (Puffin), the names of the ducklings are Jack, Kack, Lack, Mack, Nack, Ouack, Pack, and Quack. This loop outputs these names in order:

```
prefixes = "JKLMNOPQ"
suffix = "ack"

for letter in prefixes
    println(letter * suffix)
end
```

Although the output isn't quite right, because "Ouack" and "Quack" are misspelled:

```
Jack
Kack
Lack
Mack
Nack
Oack
Pack
Qack
```

Exercise 8-2

Modify the program to fix this error.

String Slices

A segment of a string is called a *slice*. Selecting a slice is similar to selecting a character:

```
julia> str = "Julius Caesar";

julia> str[1:6]
"Julius"
```

 A semicolon in REPL mode not only allows you to put multiple statements on one line but also hides the output.

The operator [*n*:*m*] returns the part of the string from the *n*th byte to the *m*th byte, so the same caution is needed as for simple indexing.

The end keyword can be used to indicate the last byte of the string:

```julia
julia> str[8:end]
"Caesar"
```

If the first index is greater than the second the result is an *empty string*, represented by two quotation marks:

```julia
julia> str[8:7]
""
```

An empty string contains no characters and has length 0, but other than that, it is the same as any other string.

Exercise 8-3

Continuing this example, what do you think str[:] means? Try it and see.

Strings Are Immutable

It is tempting to use the [ ] operator on the left side of an assignment, with the intention of changing a character in a string. For example:

```julia
julia> greeting = "Hello, world!"
"Hello, world!"
julia> greeting[1] = 'J'
ERROR: MethodError: no method matching setindex!(::String, ::Char, ::Int64)
```

The reason for the error is that strings are *immutable*, which means you can't change an existing string. The best you can do is create a new string that is a variation on the original:

```julia
julia> greeting = "J" * greeting[2:end]
"Jello, world!"
```

This example concatenates a new first letter onto a slice of greeting. It has no effect on the original string.

String Interpolation

Constructing strings using concatenation can become a bit cumbersome. To reduce the need for these verbose calls to string or repeated multiplications, Julia allows *string interpolation* using $:

```julia
julia> greet = "Hello"
"Hello"
julia> whom = "World"
"World"
```

```
julia> "$greet, $(whom)!"
"Hello, World!"
```

This is more readable and convenient than string concatenation:

```
greet * ", " * whom * "!"
```

The shortest complete expression after the $ is taken as the expression whose value is to be interpolated into the string. Thus, you can interpolate any expression into a string using parentheses:

```
julia> "1 + 2 = $(1 + 2)"
"1 + 2 = 3"
```

Searching

What does the following function do?

```
function find(word, letter)
    index = firstindex(word)
    while index <= sizeof(word)
        if word[index] == letter
            return index
        end
        index = nextind(word, index)
    end
    -1
end
```

In a sense, find is the inverse of the [] operator. Instead of taking an index and extracting the corresponding character, it takes a character and finds the index where that character appears. If the character is not found, the function returns -1.

This is the first example we have seen of a return statement inside a loop. If word[index] == letter, the function breaks out of the loop and returns immediately.

If the character doesn't appear in the string, the program exits the loop normally and returns -1.

This pattern of computation—traversing a sequence and returning when we find what we are looking for—is called a *search*.

Exercise 8-4

Modify find so that it has a third parameter, the index in word where it should start looking.

Looping and Counting

The following program counts the number of times the letter a appears in a string:

```
word = "banana"
counter = 0
for letter in word
    if letter == 'a'
        global counter = counter + 1
    end
end
println(counter)
```

This program demonstrates another pattern of computation called a *counter*. The variable counter is initialized to 0 and then incremented each time an a is found. When the loop exits, counter contains the result—the total number of a's.

Exercise 8-5

Encapsulate this code in a function named count, and generalize it so that it accepts the string and the letter as arguments.

Then rewrite the function so that instead of traversing the string, it uses the three-parameter version of find from the previous section.

String Library

Julia provides functions that perform a variety of useful operations on strings. For example, the function uppercase takes a string and returns a new string with all uppercase letters:

```
julia> uppercase("Hello, World!")
"HELLO, WORLD!"
```

As it turns out, there is a function named findfirst that is remarkably similar to the find function we wrote:

```
julia> findfirst("a", "banana")
2:2
```

Actually, the findfirst function is more general than our function; it can find substrings, not just characters:

```
julia> findfirst("na", "banana")
3:4
```

By default, findfirst starts at the beginning of the string, but the function findnext takes a third argument, the index where it should start looking:

```
julia> findnext("na", "banana", 4)
5:6
```

The ∈ Operator

The operator ∈ (`\in TAB`) is a Boolean operator that takes a character and a string and returns `true` if the first appears in the second:

```julia
julia> 'a' ∈ "banana"    # 'a' in "banana"
true
```

For example, the following function prints all the letters from `word1` that also appear in `word2`:

```julia
function inboth(word1, word2)
    for letter in word1
        if letter ∈ word2
            print(letter, " ")
        end
    end
end
```

With well-chosen variable names, Julia sometimes reads like English. You could read this loop as "for (each) letter in (the first) word, if (the) letter is an element of (the second) word, print (the) letter."

Here's what you get if you compare `"apples"` and `"oranges"`:

```julia
julia> inboth("apples", "oranges")
a e s
```

String Comparison

The relational operators work on strings. To see if two strings are equal, use `==`:

```julia
word = "Pineapple"
if word == "banana"
    println("All right, bananas.")
end
```

Other relational operations are useful for putting words in alphabetical order:

```julia
if word < "banana"
    println("Your word, $word, comes before banana.")
elseif word > "banana"
    println("Your word, $word, comes after banana.")
else
    println("All right, bananas.")
end
```

Julia does not handle uppercase and lowercase letters the same way people do. All the uppercase letters come before all the lowercase letters, so:

```julia
Your word, Pineapple, comes before banana.
```

A common way to address this problem is to convert strings to a standard format, such as all lowercase, before performing the comparison.

Debugging

When you use indices to traverse the values in a sequence, it is tricky to get the beginning and end of the traversal right. Here is a function that is supposed to compare two words and return true if one of the words is the reverse of the other, but it contains two errors:

```
function isreverse(word1, word2)
    if length(word1) != length(word2)
        return false
    end
    i = firstindex(word1)
    j = lastindex(word2)
    while j >= 0
        j = prevind(word2, j)
        if word1[i] != word2[j]
            return false
        end
        i = nextind(word1, i)
    end
    true
end
```

The first if statement checks whether the words are the same length. If not, we can return false immediately. Otherwise, for the rest of the function, we can assume that the words are the same length. This is an example of the guardian pattern; see "Checking Types" on page 72.

i and j are indices: i traverses word1 forward while j traverses word2 backward. If we find two letters that don't match, we can return false immediately. If we get through the whole loop and all the letters match, we return true.

The function lastindex returns the last valid byte index of a string and prevind finds the previous valid index of a character.

If we test this function with the words "pots" and "stop," we expect the return value true, but we get false:

```
julia> isreverse("pots", "stop")
false
```

For debugging this kind of error, my first move is to print the values of the indices:

```
while j >= 0
    j = prevind(word2, j)
```

```
@show i j
if word1[i] != word2[j]
```

Now when I run the program again, I get more information:

```
julia> isreverse("pots", "stop")
i = 1
j = 3
false
```

The first time through the loop, the value of j is 3, but it has to be 4. This can be fixed by moving j = prevind(word2, j) to the end of the while loop.

If I fix that error and run the program again, I get:

```
julia> isreverse("pots", "stop")
i = 1
j = 4
i = 2
j = 3
i = 3
j = 2
i = 4
j = 1
i = 5
j = 0
ERROR: BoundsError: attempt to access "pots"
    at index [5]
```

This time a BoundsError has been thrown. The value of i is 5, which is out of range for the string "pots".

Exercise 8-6

Run the program on paper, changing the values of i and j during each iteration. Find and fix the second error in this function.

Glossary

sequence
An ordered collection of values where each value is identified by an integer index.

ASCII standard
A character encoding standard for electronic communication specifying 128 characters.

Unicode standard
A computing industry standard for the consistent encoding, representation, and handling of text expressed in most of the world's writing systems.

index
> An integer value used to select an item in a sequence, such as a character in a string. In Julia indices start from 1.

UTF-8 encoding
> A variable-width character encoding capable of encoding all 1,112,064 valid code points in Unicode using one to four 8-bit bytes.

traverse
> To iterate through the items in a sequence, performing a similar operation on each.

slice
> A part of a string specified by a range of indices.

empty string
> A string with no characters and length 0, represented by two quotation marks.

immutable
> The property of a sequence whose items cannot be changed.

string interpolation
> The process of evaluating a string containing one or more placeholders, yielding a result in which the placeholders are replaced with their corresponding values.

search
> A pattern of traversal that stops when it finds what it is looking for.

counter
> A variable used to count something, usually initialized to zero and then incremented.

Exercises

Exercise 8-7

Read the documentation of the string functions (*http://bit.ly/2VnkAvC*). You might want to experiment with some of them to make sure you understand how they work. `strip` and `replace` are particularly useful.

The documentation uses a syntax that might be confusing. For example, in `search(string::AbstractString, chars::Chars, [start::Integer])`, the brackets indicate optional arguments. So, `string` and `chars` are required, but `start` is optional.

Exercise 8-8

There is a built-in function called `count` that is similar to the function in "Looping and Counting" on page 93. Read the documentation of this function and use it to count the number of a's in "banana".

Exercise 8-9

A string slice can take a third index. The first specifies the start, the third the end, and the second the "step size"; that is, the number of spaces between successive characters. A step size of 2 means every other character; 3 means every third, etc. For example:

```
julia> fruit = "banana"
"banana"
julia> fruit[1:2:6]
"bnn"
```

A step size of -1 goes through the word backward, so the slice [end:-1:1] generates a reversed string.

Use this idiom to write a one-line version of `ispalindrome` from "Exercise 6-6" on page 75.

Exercise 8-10

The following functions are all *intended* to check whether a string contains any lower-case letters, but at least some of them are wrong. For each function, describe what the function actually does (assuming that the parameter is a string).

```
function anylowercase1(s)
    for c in s
        if islowercase(c)
            return true
        else
            return false
        end
    end
end

function anylowercase2(s)
    for c in s
        if islowercase('c')
            return "true"
        else
            return "false"
        end
    end
end

function anylowercase3(s)
    for c in s
```

```
            flag = islowercase(c)
        end
        flag
    end

    function anylowercase4(s)
        flag = false
        for c in s
            flag = flag || islowercase(c)
        end
        flag
    end

    function anylowercase5(s)
        for c in s
            if !islowercase(c)
                return false
            end
        end
        true
    end
```

Exercise 8-11

A Caesar cypher is a weak form of encryption that involves "rotating" each letter by a fixed number of places. To rotate a letter means to shift it through the alphabet, wrapping around to the beginning if necessary, so *A* rotated by 3 is *D* and *Z* rotated by 1 is *A*.

To rotate a word, rotate each letter by the same amount. For example, "cheer" rotated by 7 is "jolly" and "melon" rotated by –10 is "cubed". In the movie *2001: A Space Odyssey*, the ship's computer is called "HAL," which is "IBM" rotated by –1.

Write a function called `rotateword` that takes a string and an integer as parameters, and returns a new string that contains the letters from the original string rotated by the given amount.

 You might want to use the built-in functions `Int`, which converts a character to a numeric code, and `Char`, which converts numeric codes to characters. Letters of the alphabet are encoded in alphabetical order, so, for example:

```
julia> Int('c') - Int('a')
2
```

because *c* is the third letter of the alphabet. But beware—the numeric codes for uppercase letters are different:

```
julia> Char(Int('A') + 32)
'a': ASCII/Unicode U+0061 (category Ll: Letter, lower case)
```

Potentially offensive jokes on the internet are sometimes encoded in ROT13, which is a Caesar cypher with rotation 13. If you are not easily offended, find and decode some of them.

CHAPTER 9

Case Study: Word Play

This chapter presents a second case study, which involves solving word puzzles by searching for words that have certain properties. For example, we'll find the longest palindromes in English and search for words whose letters appear in alphabetical order. And I will present another program development plan: reduction to a previously solved problem.

Reading Word Lists

For the exercises in this chapter we need a list of English words. There are lots of word lists available on the web, but the one most suitable for our purpose is one of the word lists collected and contributed to the public domain by Grady Ward as part of the Moby lexicon project (*http://bit.ly/2IbZfl5*). It is a list of 113,809 official crosswords; that is, words that are considered valid in crossword puzzles and other word games. In the Moby collection, the filename is *113809of.fic*; you can download a copy, with the simpler name *words.txt*, from this book's GitHub repository (*http://bit.ly/2FSlXfc*).

This file is in plain text, so you can open it with a text editor, but you can also read it from Julia. The built-in function `open` takes a name of the file as a parameter and returns a *file stream* you can use to read the file:

```julia
julia> fin = open("words.txt")
IOStream(<file words.txt>)
```

`fin` is a file stream used for input. When it is no longer needed, it has to be closed with `close(fin)`.

Julia provides several function for reading, including `readline`, which reads characters from the file until it gets to a NEWLINE and returns the result as a string:

```
julia> readline(fin)
"aa"
```

The first word in this particular list is "aa," which is a kind of lava.

The file stream keeps track of where it is in the file, so if you call `readline` again, you get the next word:

```
julia> readline(fin)
"aah"
```

The next word is "aah," which is a perfectly legitimate word, so stop looking at me like that.

You can also use a file as part of a `for` loop. This program reads *words.txt* and prints each word, one per line:

```
for line in eachline("words.txt")
    println(line)
end
```

Exercises

Exercise 9-1

Write a program that reads *words.txt* and prints only the words with more than 20 characters (not counting whitespace).

Exercise 9-2

In 1939 Ernest Vincent Wright published a 50,000-word novel called *Gadsby* (Wetzel Publishing) that does not contain the letter *e*. Since *e* is the most common letter in English, that's not easy to do.

In fact, it is difficult to construct a solitary thought without using that most common symbol. It is slow going at first, but with caution and hours of training you can gradually gain facility.

All right, I'll stop now.

Write a function called `hasno_e` that returns `true` if the given word doesn't have the letter *e* in it.

Modify your program from the previous exercise to print only the words that have no *e* and compute the percentage of the words in the list that have no *e*.

Exercise 9-3

Write a function named `avoids` that takes a word and a string of forbidden letters, and that returns `true` if the word doesn't use any of the forbidden letters.

Modify your program to prompt the user to enter a string of forbidden letters and then print the number of words that don't contain any of them. Can you find a combination of five forbidden letters that excludes the smallest number of words?

Exercise 9-4

Write a function named usesonly that takes a word and a string of letters, and that returns true if the word contains only letters in the list. Can you make a sentence using only the letters acefhlo? Other than "Hoe alfalfa"?

Exercise 9-5

Write a function named usesall that takes a word and a string of required letters, and that returns true if the word uses all the required letters at least once. How many words are there that use all the vowels aeiou? How about aeiouy?

Exercise 9-6

Write a function called isabecedarian that returns true if the letters in a word appear in alphabetical order (double letters are okay). How many abecedarian words are there?

Search

All of the exercises in the previous section have something in common; they can be solved with the search pattern. The simplest example is:

```
function hasno_e(word)
    for letter in word
        if letter == 'e'
            return false
        end
    end
    true
end
```

The for loop traverses the characters in word. If we find the letter *e*, we can immediately return false; otherwise, we have to go to the next letter. If we exit the loop normally, that means we didn't find an *e*, so we return true.

You could write this function more concisely using the ∉ (**\notin TAB**) operator, but I started with this version because it demonstrates the logic of the search pattern.

avoids is a more general version of hasno_e, but it has the same structure:

```
function avoids(word, forbidden)
    for letter in word
        if letter ∈ forbidden
            return false
```

```
            end
        end
        true
    end
```

We can return `false` as soon as we find a forbidden letter; if we get to the end of the loop, we return `true`.

`usesonly` is similar except that the sense of the condition is reversed:

```
function usesonly(word, available)
    for letter in word
        if letter ∉ available
            return false
        end
    end
    true
end
```

Instead of an array of forbidden letters, we have an array of available letters. If we find a letter in `word` that is not in `available`, we can return `false`.

`usesall` is similar except that we reverse the role of the word and the string of letters:

```
function usesall(word, required)
    for letter in required
        if letter ∉ word
            return false
        end
    end
    true
end
```

Instead of traversing the letters in `word`, the loop traverses the required letters. If any of the required letters do not appear in `word`, we can return `false`.

If you were really thinking like a computer scientist, you would have recognized that `usesall` was an instance of a previously solved problem, and you would have written:

```
function usesall(word, required)
    usesonly(required, word)
end
```

This is an example of a program development plan called *reduction to a previously solved problem*, which means that you recognize the problem you are working on as an instance of a solved problem and apply an existing solution.

Looping with Indices

I wrote the functions in the previous section with `for` loops because I only needed the characters in the strings; I didn't have to do anything with the indices.

For `isabecedarian` we have to compare adjacent letters, which is a little tricky with a for loop:

```
function isabecedarian(word)
    i = firstindex(word)
    previous = word[i]
    j = nextind(word, i)
    for c in word[j:end]
        if c < previous
            return false
        end
        previous = c
    end
    true
end
```

An alternative is to use recursion:

```
function isabecedarian(word)
    if length(word) <= 1
        return true
    end
    i = firstindex(word)
    j = nextind(word, i)
    if word[i] > word[j]
        return false
    end
    isabecedarian(word[j:end])
end
```

Another option is to use a `while` loop:

```
function isabecedarian(word)
    i = firstindex(word)
    j = nextind(word, 1)
    while j <= sizeof(word)
        if word[j] < word[i]
            return false
        end
        i = j
        j = nextind(word, i)
    end
    true
end
```

The loop starts at `i=1` and `j=nextind(word, 1)` and ends when `j>sizeof(word)`. Each time through the loop, it compares the `i`th character (which you can think of as the current character) to the `j`th character (which you can think of as the next).

If the next character is less than (alphabetically before) the current one, then we have discovered a break in the abecedarian trend, and we return `false`.

If we get to the end of the loop without finding a fault, then the word passes the test. To convince yourself that the loop ends correctly, consider an example like "flossy".

Here is a version of ispalindrome that uses two indices; one starts at the beginning and goes up, and the other starts at the end and goes down:

```
function ispalindrome(word)
    i = firstindex(word)
    j = lastindex(word)
    while i<j
        if word[i] != word[j]
            return false
        end
        i = nextind(word, i)
        j = prevind(word, j)
    end
    true
end
```

Or we could reduce to a previously solved problem and write

```
function ispalindrome(word)
    isreverse(word, word)
end
```

using isreverse from "Debugging" on page 95.

Debugging

Testing programs is hard. The functions in this chapter are relatively easy to test because you can check the results by hand. Even so, it is somewhere between difficult and impossible to choose a set of words that tests for all possible errors.

Taking hasno_e as an example, there are two obvious cases to check: words that have an *e* should return false, and words that don't should return true. You should have no trouble coming up with one of each.

Within each case, there are some less obvious subcases. Among the words that have an *e*, you should test words with an *e* at the beginning, the end, and somewhere in the middle. You should test long words, short words, and very short words, like the empty string. The empty string is an example of a *special case*, which is one of the nonobvious cases where errors often lurk.

In addition to the test cases you generate, you can also test your program with a word list like *words.txt*. By scanning the output, you might be able to catch errors, but be careful: you might catch one kind of error (words that should not be included, but are) and not another (words that should be included, but aren't).

In general, testing can help you find bugs, but it is not easy to generate a good set of test cases, and even if you do, you can't be sure your program is correct. According to a legendary computer scientist:

> Program testing can be used to show the presence of bugs, but never to show their absence!
>
> —Edsger W. Dijkstra

Glossary

file stream
A value that represents an open file.

reduction to a previously solved problem
A way of solving a problem by expressing it as an instance of a previously solved problem.

special case
A test case that is atypical or nonobvious (and less likely to be handled correctly).

Exercises

Exercise 9-7

This question is based on a Puzzler that was broadcast on the radio program *Car Talk* (*http://bit.ly/2OM2Fwp*):

> Give me a word with three consecutive double letters. I'll give you a couple of words that almost qualify, but don't. For example, the word committee, c-o-m-m-i-t-t-e-e. It would be great except for the i that sneaks in there. Or Mississippi—M-i-s-s-i-s-s-i-p-p-i. If you could take out those i's it would work. But there is a word that has three consecutive pairs of letters and to the best of my knowledge this may be the only word. Of course there are probably 500 more but I can only think of one. What is the word?

Write a program to find it.

Exercise 9-8

Here's another *Car Talk* Puzzler:

> I was driving on the highway the other day recently and I happened to notice my odometer. Like most odometers nowadays, it shows six digits, in whole miles only—no tenths of a mile. So, if my car had 300,000 miles, for example, I'd see 3-0-0-0-0-0. ...
>
> Now, what I saw that day was very interesting. I noticed that the last 4 digits were palindromic, that is they read the same forwards as backwards. For example, "5-4-4-5" is a palindrome. So my odometer could have read 3-1-5-4-4-5 ... .

One mile later, the last 5 numbers were palindromic. For example, it could have read 3-6-5-4-5-6.

One mile after that, the middle 4 out of 6 numbers were palindromic. … And you ready for this? One mile later, all 6 were palindromic! …

The question is, what did [I] see on the odometer when [I] first looked?

Write a Julia program that tests all the six-digit numbers and prints any numbers that satisfy these requirements.

Exercise 9-9

Here's a third *Car Talk* Puzzler that you can solve with a search:

Recently I had a visit with my mom and we realized that the two digits that make up my age when reversed result in her age. For example, if she's 73, I'm 37. We wondered how often this has happened over the years but we got sidetracked with other topics and we never came up with an answer.

When I got home I figured out that the digits of our ages have been reversible six times so far. I also figured out that if we're lucky it would happen again in a few years, and if we're really lucky it would happen one more time after that. In other words, it would have happened 8 times over all. So the question is, how old am I now?

Write a Julia program that searches for solutions to this Puzzler.

 You might find the function lpad useful.

CHAPTER 10

Arrays

This chapter presents one of Julia's most useful built-in types, the array. You will also learn about objects and what can happen when you have more than one name for the same object.

An Array Is a Sequence

Like a string, an *array* is a sequence of values. In a string, the values are characters; in an array, they can be any type. The values in an array are called *elements* or sometimes *items*.

There are several ways to create a new array; the simplest is to enclose the elements in square brackets ([ ]):

```
[10, 20, 30, 40]
["crunchy frog", "ram bladder", "lark vomit"]
```

The first example is an array of four integers. The second is an array of three strings. The elements of an array don't have to be the same type. The following array contains a string, a float, an integer, and another array:

```
["spam", 2.0, 5, [10, 20]]
```

An array within another array is *nested*.

An array that contains no elements is called an empty array; you can create one with empty brackets, [ ].

As you might expect, you can assign array values to variables:

```
julia> cheeses = ["Cheddar", "Edam", "Gouda"];

julia> numbers = [42, 123];
```

```
julia> empty = [];

julia> print(cheeses, " ", numbers, " ", empty)
["Cheddar", "Edam", "Gouda"] [42, 123] Any[]
```

The function typeof can be used to find out the type of the array:

```
julia> typeof(cheeses)
Array{String,1}
julia> typeof(numbers)
Array{Int64,1}
julia> typeof(empty)
Array{Any,1}
```

The number indicates the dimensions (we'll talk more about this in "Arrays" on page 241). The array empty contains values of type Any; that is, it can hold values of all types.

Arrays Are Mutable

The syntax for accessing the elements of an array is the same as for accessing the characters of a string—using the bracket operator. The expression inside the brackets specifies the index. Remember that the indices start at 1:

```
julia> cheeses[1]
"Cheddar"
```

Unlike strings, arrays are *mutable*; that is, their values can be changed. When the bracket operator appears on the left side of an assignment, it identifies the element of the array that will be assigned:

```
julia> numbers[2] = 5
5
julia> print(numbers)
[42, 5]
```

The second element of numbers, which used to be 123, is now 5.

Figure 10-1 shows the state diagrams for cheeses, numbers, and empty.

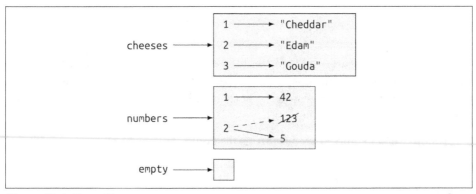

Figure 10-1. State diagram

Arrays are represented by boxes with the elements of the array inside them. cheeses refers to an array with three elements indexed: 1, 2, and 3. numbers contains two elements; the diagram shows that the value of the second element has been reassigned from 123 to 5. empty refers to an array with no elements.

Array indices work the same way as string indices (but without UTF-8 caveats):

- Any integer expression can be used as an index.
- If you try to read or write an element that does not exist, you get a BoundsError.
- The keyword end points to the last index of the array.

The ∈ operator also works on arrays:

```
julia> "Edam" ∈ cheeses
true
julia> "Brie" in cheeses
false
```

Traversing an Array

The most common way to traverse the elements of an array is with a for loop. The syntax is the same as for strings:

```
for cheese in cheeses
    println(cheese)
end
```

This works well if you only need to read the elements of the array. But if you want to write or update the elements, you need the indices. One technique is to use the built-in function eachindex:

```
for i in eachindex(numbers)
    numbers[i] = numbers[i] * 2
end
```

This loop traverses the array and updates each element. length returns the number of elements in the array. Each time through the loop i gets the index of the next element. The assignment statement in the body uses i to read the old value of the element and to assign the new value.

A for loop over an empty array never runs the body:

```
for x in []
    println("This can never happen.")
end
```

Although an array can contain another array, the nested array still counts as a single element. The length of this array is 4:

```
["spam", 1, ["Brie", "Roquefort", "Camembert"], [1, 2, 3]]
```

Array Slices

The slice operator ([*n*:_*m*_]) also works on arrays:

```
julia> t = ['a', 'b', 'c', 'd', 'e', 'f'];

julia> print(t[1:3])
['a', 'b', 'c']
julia> print(t[3:end])
['c', 'd', 'e', 'f']
```

Using the slice operator without arguments makes a copy of the whole array:

```
julia> print(t[:])
['a', 'b', 'c', 'd', 'e', 'f']
```

Since arrays are mutable, it is often useful to make a copy before performing operations that modify arrays.

A slice operator on the left side of an assignment can update multiple elements:

```
julia> t[2:3] = ['x', 'y'];

julia> print(t)
['a', 'x', 'y', 'd', 'e', 'f']
```

Array Library

Julia provides functions that operate on arrays. For example, push! adds a new element to the end of an array:

```
julia> t = ['a', 'b', 'c'];

julia> push!(t, 'd');

julia> print(t)
['a', 'b', 'c', 'd']
```

append! adds the elements of the second array to the end of the first:

```
julia> t1 = ['a', 'b', 'c'];

julia> t2 = ['d', 'e'];

julia> append!(t1, t2);

julia> print(t1)
['a', 'b', 'c', 'd', 'e']
```

This example leaves t2 unmodified.

sort! arranges the elements of the array from low to high:

```
julia> t = ['d', 'c', 'e', 'b', 'a'];

julia> sort!(t);

julia> print(t)
['a', 'b', 'c', 'd', 'e']
```

sort returns a copy of the elements of the array in order:

```
julia> t1 = ['d', 'c', 'e', 'b', 'a'];

julia> t2 = sort(t1);

julia> print(t1)
['d', 'c', 'e', 'b', 'a']
julia> print(t2)
['a', 'b', 'c', 'd', 'e']
```

 As a style convention in Julia, ! is appended to names of functions that modify their arguments.

Map, Filter, and Reduce

To add up all the numbers in an array, you can use a loop like this:

```
function addall(t)
    total = 0
    for x in t
```

```
        total += x
    end
    total
end
```

`total` is initialized to 0. Each time through the loop, `+=` gets one element from the array. The `+=` operator provides a short way to update a variable. This *augmented assignment statement*:

```
total += x
```

is equivalent to:

```
total = total + x
```

As the loop runs, `total` accumulates the sum of the elements; a variable used this way is sometimes called an *accumulator*.

Adding up the elements of an array is such a common operation that Julia provides it as a built-in function, `sum`:

```
julia> t = [1, 2, 3, 4];

julia> sum(t)
10
```

An operation like this that combines a sequence of elements into a single value is sometimes called a *reduce operation*.

Often you want to traverse one array while building another. For example, the following function takes an array of strings and returns a new array that contains capitalized strings:

```
function capitalizeall(t)
    res = []
    for s in t
        push!(res, uppercase(s))
    end
    res
end
```

`res` is initialized with an empty array; each time through the loop, we append the next element. So, `res` is another kind of accumulator.

An operation like `capitalizeall` is sometimes called a *map* because it "maps" a function (in this case `uppercase`) onto each of the elements in a sequence.

Another common operation is to select some of the elements from an array and return a subarray. For example, the following function takes an array of strings and returns an array that contains only the uppercase strings:

```
function onlyupper(t)
    res = []
```

```
        for s in t
            if s == uppercase(s)
                push!(res, s)
            end
        end
        res
    end
```

An operation like onlyupper is called a *filter* because it selects some of the elements and filters out the others.

Most common array operations can be expressed as a combination of map, filter, and reduce.

Dot Syntax

For every binary operator, like ^, there is a corresponding *dot operator*, like .^, that is automatically defined to perform the operation element-by-element on arrays. For example, [1, 2, 3] ^ 3 is not defined, but [1, 2, 3] .^ 3 is defined as computing the elementwise result [1^3, 2^3, 3^3]:

```
julia> print([1, 2, 3] .^ 3)
[1, 8, 27]
```

Any Julia function *f* can be applied elementwise to any array with the *dot syntax*. For example, to capitalize an array of strings, we don't need an explicit loop:

```
julia> t = uppercase.(["abc", "def", "ghi"]);

julia> print(t)
["ABC", "DEF", "GHI"]
```

This is an elegant way to create a map. The function capitalizeall can be implemented by a one-liner:

```
function capitalizeall(t)
    uppercase.(t)
end
```

Deleting (Inserting) Elements

There are several ways to delete elements from an array. If you know the index of the element you want, you can use splice!:

```
julia> t = ['a', 'b', 'c'];

julia> splice!(t, 2)
'b': ASCII/Unicode U+0062 (category Ll: Letter, lowercase)
julia> print(t)
['a', 'c']
```

`splice!` modifies the array and returns the element that was removed.

`pop!` deletes and returns the last element:

```
julia> t = ['a', 'b', 'c'];

julia> pop!(t)
'c': ASCII/Unicode U+0063 (category Ll: Letter, lowercase)
julia> print(t)
['a', 'b']
```

`popfirst!` deletes and returns the first element:

```
julia> t = ['a', 'b', 'c'];

julia> popfirst!(t)
'a': ASCII/Unicode U+0061 (category Ll: Letter, lowercase)
julia> print(t)
['b', 'c']
```

The functions `pushfirst!` and `push!` insert an element at the beginning and end, respectively, of the array.

If you don't need the removed value, you can use the function `deleteat!`:

```
julia> t = ['a', 'b', 'c'];

julia> print(deleteat!(t, 2))
['a', 'c']
```

The function `insert!` inserts an element at a given index:

```
julia> t = ['a', 'b', 'c'];

julia> print(insert!(t, 2, 'x'))
['a', 'x', 'b', 'c']
```

Arrays and Strings

A string is a sequence of characters and an array is a sequence of values, but an array of characters is not the same as a string. To convert from a string to an array of characters, you can use the function `collect`:

```
julia> t = collect("spam");

julia> print(t)
['s', 'p', 'a', 'm']
```

The `collect` function breaks a string or another sequence into individual elements.

If you want to break a string into words, you can use the `split` function:

```
julia> t = split("pining for the fjords");
```

```
julia> print(t)
SubString{String}["pining", "for", "the", "fjords"]
```

An *optional argument* called a *delimiter* specifies which characters to use as word boundaries (we talked briefly about optional arguments in "Exercise 8-7" on page 97). The following example uses a hyphen as a delimiter:

```
julia> t = split("spam-spam-spam", '-');
```

```
julia> print(t)
SubString{String}["spam", "spam", "spam"]
```

`join` is the inverse of `split`. It takes an array of strings and concatenates the elements:

```
julia> t = ["pining", "for", "the", "fjords"];
```

```
julia> s = join(t, ' ')
"pining for the fjords"
```

In this case the delimiter is a space character. To concatenate strings without spaces, you don't specify a delimiter.

Objects and Values

An *object* is something a variable can refer to. Until now, you might have used "object" and "value" interchangeably.

If we run these assignment statements:

```
a = "banana"
b = "banana"
```

we know that a and b both refer to a string, but we don't know whether they refer to the *same* string. There are two possible states, as shown in Figure 10-2.

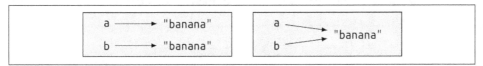

Figure 10-2. State diagrams

In one case, a and b refer to two different objects that have the same value. In the second case, they refer to the same object.

To check whether two variables refer to the same object, you can use the ≡ (**\equiv TAB**) or === operator:

```
julia> a = "banana"
"banana"
julia> b = "banana"
```

```
"banana"
julia> a ≡ b
true
```

In this example, Julia only created one string object, and both a and b refer to it. But when you create two arrays, you get two objects:

```
julia> a = [1, 2, 3];

julia> b = [1, 2, 3];

julia> a ≡ b
false
```

So the state diagram looks like Figure 10-3.

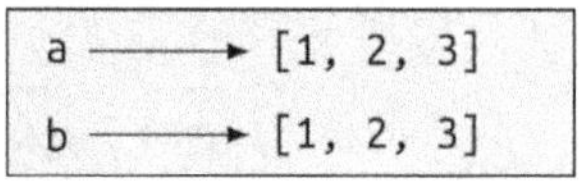

Figure 10-3. State diagram

In this case we would say that the two arrays are *equivalent*, because they have the same elements, but not *identical*, because they are not the same object. If two objects are identical, they are also equivalent, but if they are equivalent, they are not necessarily identical.

To be precise, an object has a value. If you evaluate [1, 2, 3], you get an array object whose value is a sequence of integers. If another array has the same elements, we say it has the same value, but it is not the same object.

Aliasing

If a refers to an object and you assign b = a, then both variables refer to the same object:

```
julia> a = [1, 2, 3];

julia> b = a;

julia> b ≡ a
true
```

The state diagram looks like Figure 10-4.

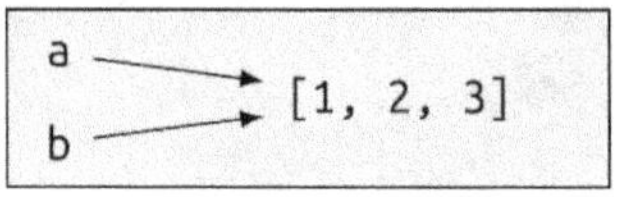

Figure 10-4. State diagram

The association of a variable with an object is called a *reference*. In this example, there are two references to the same object.

An object with more than one reference has more than one name, so we say that the object is *aliased*.

If the aliased object is mutable, changes made with one alias affect the other:

```
julia> b[1] = 42
42
julia> print(a)
[42, 2, 3]
```

 Although this behavior can be useful, it is error-prone. In general, it is safer to avoid aliasing when you are working with mutable objects.

For immutable objects like strings, aliasing is not as much of a problem. In this example:

```
a = "banana"
b = "banana"
```

it almost never makes a difference whether a and b refer to the same string or not.

Array Arguments

When you pass an array to a function, the function gets a reference to the array. If the function modifies the array, the caller sees the change. For example, deletehead! removes the first element from an array:

```
function deletehead!(t)
    popfirst!(t)
end
```

Here's how it is used:

```
julia> letters = ['a', 'b', 'c'];

julia> deletehead!(letters);

julia> print(letters)
['b', 'c']
```

The parameter t and the variable letters are aliases for the same object. The stack diagram looks like Figure 10-5.

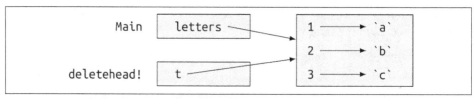

Figure 10-5. Stack diagram

Since the array is shared by two frames, I drew it between them.

It is important to distinguish between operations that modify arrays and operations that create new arrays. For example, push! modifies an array, but vcat creates a new array.

Here's an example using push!:

```
julia> t1 = [1, 2];

julia> t2 = push!(t1, 3);

julia> print(t1)
[1, 2, 3]
```

t2 is an alias of t1.

Here's an example using vcat:

```
julia> t3 = vcat(t1, [4]);

julia> print(t1)
[1, 2, 3]
julia> print(t3)
[1, 2, 3, 4]
```

The result of vcat is a new array, and the original array is unchanged.

This difference is important when you write functions that are supposed to modify arrays.

For example, this function *does not* delete the head of an array:

```
function baddeletehead(t)
    t = t[2:end]              # WRONG!
end
```

The slice operator creates a new array and the assignment makes t refer to it, but that doesn't affect the caller:

```
julia> t4 = baddeletehead(t3);

julia> print(t3)
[1, 2, 3, 4]
```

```
julia> print(t4)
[2, 3, 4]
```

At the beginning of `baddeletehead`, `t` and `t3` refer to the same array. At the end, `t` refers to a new array, but `t3` still refers to the original unmodified array.

An alternative is to write a function that creates and returns a new array. For example, `tail` returns all but the first element of an array:

```
function tail(t)
    t[2:end]
end
```

This function leaves the original array unmodified. Here's how it is used:

```
julia> letters = ['a', 'b', 'c'];

julia> rest = tail(letters);

julia> print(rest)
['b', 'c']
```

Debugging

Careless use of arrays (and other mutable objects) can lead to long hours of debugging. Here are some common pitfalls and ways to avoid them:

- Most array functions modify the argument. This is the opposite of the string functions, which return a new string and leave the original alone.

  If you are used to writing string code like this:

  ```
  new_word = strip(word)
  ```

  It is tempting to write array code like this:

  ```
  t2 = sort!(t1)
  ```

  Because `sort!` returns the modified original array `t1`, `t2` is an alias of `t1`.

   Before using array functions and operators, you should read the documentation carefully and then test them in interactive mode.

- Pick an idiom and stick with it.

  Part of the problem with arrays is that there are too many ways to do things. For example, to remove an element from an array, you can use `pop!`, `popfirst!`, `delete_at`, or even a slice assignment. To add an element, you can use `push!`, pushfirst!, insert!, or vcat. Assuming that t is an array and x is an array element, these are correct:

```
insert!(t, 4, x)
push!(t, x)
append!(t, [x])
```

And these are wrong:

```
insert!(t, 4, [x])      # WRONG!
push!(t, [x])           # WRONG!
vcat(t, [x])            # WRONG!
```

- Make copies to avoid aliasing.

  If you want to use a function like sort! that modifies the argument, but you need to keep the original array as well, you can make a copy:

```
julia> t = [3, 1, 2];

julia> t2 = t[:]; # t2 = copy(t)

julia> sort!(t2);

julia> print(t)
[3, 1, 2]
julia> print(t2)
[1, 2, 3]
```

  In this example you could also use the built-in function sort, which returns a new sorted array and leaves the original alone:

```
julia> t2 = sort(t);

julia> println(t)
[3, 1, 2]
julia> println(t2)
[1, 2, 3]
```

Glossary

array
   A sequence of values.

element
   One of the values in an array (or other sequence); also called *items*.

nested array
   An array that is an element of another array.

mutable

The property of a value that can be modified.

augmented assignment

A statement that updates the value of a variable using an operator like =.

accumulator

A variable used in a loop to add up or accumulate a result.

reduce operation

A processing pattern that traverses a sequence and accumulates the elements into a single result.

map

A processing pattern that traverses a sequence and performs an operation on each element.

filter

A processing pattern that traverses a sequence and selects the elements that satisfy some criterion.

dot operator

A binary operator that is applied element-by-element to arrays.

dot syntax

Syntax used to apply a function elementwise to any array.

optional argument

An argument that is not required.

delimiter

A character or string used to indicate where a string should be split.

object

Something a variable can refer to. An object has a type and a value.

equivalent

Having the same value.

identical

Being the same object (which implies equivalence).

reference

The association between a variable and its value.

aliasing

A circumstance where two or more variables refer to the same object.

Exercises

Exercise 10-1

Write a function called nestedsum that takes an array of arrays of integers and adds up the elements from all of the nested arrays. For example:

```julia
julia> t = [[1, 2], [3], [4, 5, 6]];

julia> nestedsum(t)
21
```

Exercise 10-2

Write a function called cumulsum that takes an array of numbers and returns the cumulative sum; that is, a new array where the ith element is the sum of the first i elements from the original array. For example:

```julia
julia> t = [1, 2, 3];

julia> print(cumulsum(t))
Any[1, 3, 6]
```

Exercise 10-3

Write a function called interior that takes an array and returns a new array that contains all but the first and last elements. For example:

```julia
julia> t = [1, 2, 3, 4];

julia> print(interior(t))
[2, 3]
```

Exercise 10-4

Write a function called interior! that takes an array, modifies it by removing the first and last elements, and returns nothing. For example:

```julia
julia> t = [1, 2, 3, 4];

julia> interior!(t)

julia> print(t)
[2, 3]
```

Exercise 10-5

Write a function called issort that takes an array as a parameter and returns true if the array is sorted in ascending order and false otherwise. For example:

```
julia> issort([1, 2, 2])
true
julia> issort(['b', 'a'])
false
```

Exercise 10-6

Two words are anagrams if you can rearrange the letters from one to spell the other.
Write a function called isanagram that takes two strings and returns true if they are
anagrams.

Exercise 10-7

Write a function called hasduplicates that takes an array and returns true if there is
any element that appears more than once. It should not modify the original array.

Exercise 10-8

This exercise pertains to the so-called Birthday Paradox (*http://bit.ly/2WLJbuE*).

If there are 23 students in your class, what are the chances that 2 of you have the same
birthday? You can estimate this probability by generating random samples of 23
birthdays and checking for matches.

You can generate random birthdays with rand(1:365).

Exercise 10-9

Write two versions of a function that reads the file *words.txt* and builds an array with
one element per word, one using push! and the other using the idiom t = [t...,
x]. Which one takes longer to run? Why?

Exercise 10-10

To check whether a word is in the word array you just built, you could use the ∈ operator, but it would be slow because it searches through the words in order.

Because the words are in alphabetical order, we can speed things up with a bisection
search (also known as a binary search), which is similar to what you do when you
look a word up in the dictionary. You start in the middle and check to see whether the
word you are looking for comes before the word in the middle of the array. If so, you
search the first half of the array the same way. Otherwise, you search the second half.

Either way, you cut the remaining search space in half. If the word array has 113,809 words, it will take about 17 steps to find the word or conclude that it's not there.

Write a function called `inbisect` that takes a sorted array and a target value and returns `true` if the word is in the array and `false` if it's not.

Exercise 10-11

Two words are a "reverse pair" if each is the reverse of the other. Write a function `reversepairs` that finds all the reverse pairs in the word array.

Exercise 10-12

Two words "interlock" if taking alternating letters from each forms a new word. For example, "shoe" and "cold" interlock to form "schooled."

1. Write a program that finds all pairs of words that interlock.

 Don't enumerate all pairs!

   Credit: This exercise is inspired by an example at *http://puzzlers.org*.

2. Can you find any words that are three-way interlocked (i.e., every third letter forms a word, starting from the first, second, or third letter)?

CHAPTER 11

Dictionaries

This chapter presents another built-in type called a dictionary.

A Dictionary Is a Mapping

A *dictionary* is like an array, but more general. In an array, the indices have to be integers; in a dictionary they can be (almost) any type.

A dictionary contains a collection of indices, which are called *keys*, and a collection of *values*. Each key is associated with a single value. The association of a key and a value is called a *key-value pair*, or sometimes an *item*.

In mathematical language, a dictionary represents a *mapping* from keys to values, so you can also say that each key "maps to" a value. As an example, we'll build a dictionary that maps from English to Spanish words, so the keys and the values are all strings.

The function `Dict` creates a new dictionary with no items (because `Dict` is the name of a built-in function, you should avoid using it as a variable name):

```
julia> eng2sp = Dict()
Dict{Any,Any} with 0 entries
```

The types of the keys and values in the dictionary are specified in curly braces: here, both are of type `Any`.

The dictionary is empty. To add items to the dictionary, you can use square brackets:

```
julia> eng2sp["one"] = "uno";
```

This line creates an item that maps from the key `"one"` to the value `"uno"`. If we print the dictionary again, we see a key-value pair with an arrow `=>` between the key and value:

```
julia> eng2sp
Dict{Any,Any} with 1 entry:
  "one" => "uno"
```

This output format is also an input format. For example, you can create a new dictionary with three items as follows:

```
julia> eng2sp = Dict("one" => "uno", "two" => "dos", "three" => "tres")
Dict{String,String} with 3 entries:
  "two"   => "dos"
  "one"   => "uno"
  "three" => "tres"
```

Here all the initial keys and values are strings, so a `Dict{String,String}` is created.

The order of the items in a dictionary is unpredictable. If you type the same example on your computer, you might get a different result.

But that's not a problem because the elements of a dictionary are never indexed with integer indices. Instead, you use the keys to look up the corresponding values:

```
julia> eng2sp["two"]
"dos"
```

The key `"two"` always maps to the value `"dos"`, so the order of the items doesn't matter.

If the key isn't in the dictionary, you get an exception:

```
julia> eng2sp["four"]
ERROR: KeyError: key "four" not found
```

The `length` function works on dictionaries; it returns the number of key-value pairs:

```
julia> length(eng2sp)
3
```

The function `keys` returns a collection with the keys of the dictionary:

```
julia> ks = keys(eng2sp);

julia> print(ks)
["two", "one", "three"]
```

Now you can use the ∈ operator to see whether something appears as a key in the dictionary:

```
julia> "one" ∈ ks
true
julia> "uno" ∈ ks
false
```

To see whether something appears as a value in a dictionary, you can use the function `values`, which returns a collection of values, and then use the ∈ operator:

```
julia> vs = values(eng2sp);

julia> "uno" ∈ vs
true
```

The ∈ operator uses different algorithms for arrays and dictionaries. For arrays, it searches the elements of the array in order, as described in "Searching" on page 92. As the array gets longer, the search time gets longer in direct proportion.

For dictionaries, Julia uses an algorithm called a *hash table* that has a remarkable property: the ∈ operator takes about the same amount of time no matter how many items are in the dictionary.

Dictionaries as Collections of Counters

Suppose you are given a string and you want to count how many times each letter appears. There are several ways you could do it:

- You could create 26 variables, one for each letter of the alphabet. Then you could traverse the string and, for each character, increment the corresponding counter, probably using a chained conditional.

- You could create an array with 26 elements. Then you could convert each character to a number (using the built-in function Int), use the number as an index into the array, and increment the appropriate counter.

- You could create a dictionary with characters as keys and counters as the corresponding values. The first time you see a character, you would add an item to the dictionary. After that you would increment the value of an existing item.

Each of these options performs the same computation, but each of them implements that computation in a different way.

An *implementation* is a way of performing a computation. Some implementations are better than others. For example, an advantage of the dictionary implementation is that we don't have to know ahead of time which letters appear in the string and we only have to make room for the letters that do appear.

Here is what the code might look like:

```
function histogram(s)
    d = Dict()
    for c in s
        if c ∉ keys(d)
            d[c] = 1
        else
            d[c] += 1
        end
    end
end
```

```
        d
    end
```

The name of the function is `histogram`, which is a statistical term for a collection of counters (or frequencies).

The first line of the function creates an empty dictionary. The `for` loop traverses the string. Each time through the loop, if the character `c` is not in the dictionary, we create a new item with key `c` and the initial value 1 (since we have seen this letter once). If `c` is already in the dictionary we increment `d[c]`.

Here's how it works:

```
julia> h = histogram("brontosaurus")
Dict{Any,Any} with 8 entries:
  'n' => 1
  's' => 2
  'a' => 1
  'r' => 2
  't' => 1
  'o' => 2
  'u' => 2
  'b' => 1
```

The histogram indicates that the letters *a* and *b* appear once, *o* appears twice, and so on.

Dictionaries have a function called `get` that takes a key and a default value. If the key appears in the dictionary, `get` returns the corresponding value; otherwise, it returns the default value. For example:

```
julia> h = histogram("a")
Dict{Any,Any} with 1 entry:
  'a' => 1
julia> get(h, 'a', 0)
1
julia> get(h, 'b', 0)
0
```

Exercise 11-1

Use `get` to write `histogram` more concisely. You should be able to eliminate the `if` statement.

Looping and Dictionaries

You can traverse the keys of a dictionary in a `for` statement. For example, `printhist` prints each key and the corresponding value:

```
function printhist(h)
    for c in keys(h)
```

```
            println(c, " ", h[c])
        end
    end
```

Here's what the output looks like:

```
julia> h = histogram("parrot");

julia> printhist(h)
a 1
r 2
p 1
o 1
t 1
```

Again, the keys are in no particular order. To traverse the keys in sorted order, you can combine sort and collect:

```
julia> for c in sort(collect(keys(h)))
           println(c, " ", h[c])
       end
a 1
o 1
p 1
r 2
t 1
```

Reverse Lookup

Given a dictionary d and a key k, it is easy to find the corresponding value v = d[k]. This operation is called a *lookup*.

But what if you have v and you want to find k? You have two problems. First, there might be more than one key that maps to the value v. Depending on the application, you might be able to pick one, or you might have to make an array that contains all of them. Second, there is no simple syntax to do a *reverse lookup*; you have to search.

A reverse lookup is much slower than a forward lookup; if you have to do it often, or if the dictionary gets big, the performance of your program will suffer.

Here is a function that takes a value and returns the first key that maps to that value:

```
function reverselookup(d, v)
    for k in keys(d)
        if d[k] == v
            return k
        end
    end
```

```
        error("LookupError")
    end
```

This function is yet another example of the search pattern, but it uses a function we haven't seen before: `error`. The `error` function is used to produce an `ErrorException` that interrupts the normal flow of control. In this case it has the message `"LookupError"`, indicating that a key does not exist.

If we get to the end of the loop, that means v doesn't appear in the dictionary as a value, so we throw an exception.

Here is an example of a successful reverse lookup:

```
julia> h = histogram("parrot");

julia> key = reverselookup(h, 2)
'r': ASCII/Unicode U+0072 (category Ll: Letter, lowercase)
```

And an unsuccessful one:

```
julia> key = reverselookup(h, 3)
ERROR: LookupError
```

The effect when you generate an exception is the same as when Julia throws one: it prints a stacktrace and an error message.

 Julia provides an optimized way to do a reverse lookup: `findall(isequal(3), h)`.

Dictionaries and Arrays

Arrays can appear as values in a dictionary. For example, if you are given a dictionary that maps from letters to frequencies, you might want to invert it—that is, create a dictionary that maps from frequencies to letters. Since there might be several letters with the same frequency, each value in the inverted dictionary should be an array of letters.

Here is a function that inverts a dictionary:

```
function invertdict(d)
    inverse = Dict()
    for key in keys(d)
        val = d[key]
        if val ∉ keys(inverse)
            inverse[val] = [key]
        else
            push!(inverse[val], key)
        end
```

```
      end
      inverse
   end
```

Each time through the loop, `key` gets a key from d and `val` gets the corresponding value. If `val` is not in `inverse`, that means we haven't seen it before, so we create a new item and initialize it with a *singleton* (an array that contains a single element). Otherwise, we have seen this value before, so we append the corresponding key to the array.

Here is an example:

```
julia> hist = histogram("parrot");

julia> inverse = invertdict(hist)
Dict{Any,Any} with 2 entries:
  2 => ['r']
  1 => ['a', 'p', 'o', 't']
```

Figure 11-1 is a state diagram showing `hist` and `inverse`. A dictionary is represented as a box with the key-value pairs inside. If the values are integers, floats, or strings, I draw them inside the box, but I usually draw arrays outside the box, just to keep the diagram simple.

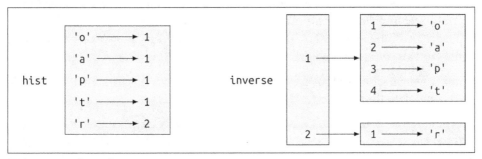

Figure 11-1. State diagram

I mentioned earlier that a dictionary is implemented using a hash table. That means that the keys have to be *hashable*.

A *hash* is a function that takes a value (of any kind) and returns an integer. Dictionaries use these integers, called hash values, to store and look up key-value pairs.

Memos

If you played with the `fibonacci` function from "One More Example" on page 71, you might have noticed that the bigger the argument you provide, the longer the function takes to run. Furthermore, the runtime increases quickly.

To understand why, consider Figure 11-2, which shows the *call graph* for fibonacci with n = 4.

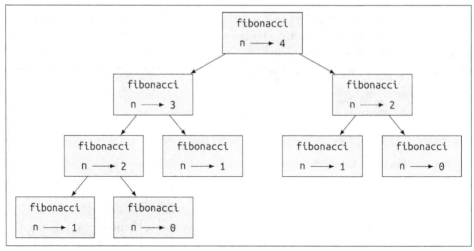

Figure 11-2. Call graph

A call graph shows a set of function frames, with lines connecting each frame to the frames of the functions it calls. At the top of the graph, fibonacci with n = 4 calls fibonacci with n = 3 and n = 2. In turn, fibonacci with n = 3 calls fibonacci with n = 2 and n = 1, and so on.

Count how many times fibonacci(0) and fibonacci(1) are called. This is an inefficient solution to the problem, and it gets worse as the argument gets bigger.

One solution is to keep track of values that have already been computed by storing them in a dictionary. A previously computed value that is stored for later use is called a *memo*. Here is a "memoized" version of fibonacci:

```
known = Dict(0=>0, 1=>1)

function fibonacci(n)
    if n ∈ keys(known)
        return known[n]
    end
    res = fibonacci(n-1) + fibonacci(n-2)
    known[n] = res
    res
end
```

known is a dictionary that keeps track of the Fibonacci numbers we already know. It starts with two items: 0 maps to 0 and 1 maps to 1.

Whenever `fibonacci` is called, it checks `known`. If the result is already there, it can return immediately. Otherwise, it has to compute the new value, add it to the dictionary, and return it.

If you run this version of `fibonacci` and compare it with the original, you will find that it is much faster.

Global Variables

In the previous example, `known` is created outside the function, so it belongs to the special frame called `Main`. Variables in `Main` are sometimes called *global* because they can be accessed from any function. Unlike local variables, which disappear when their function ends, global variables persist from one function call to the next.

It is common to use global variables for *flags*; that is, Boolean variables that indicate ("flag") whether a condition is true. For example, some programs use a flag named `verbose` to control the level of detail in the output:

```
verbose = true

function example1()
    if verbose
        println("Running example1")
    end
end
```

If you try to reassign a global variable, you might be surprised. The following example is supposed to keep track of whether the function has been called:

```
been_called = false

function example2()
    been_called = true        # WRONG
end
```

But if you run it you will see that the value of `been_called` doesn't change. The problem is that `example2` creates a new local variable named `been_called`. The local variable goes away when the function ends, and has no effect on the global variable.

To reassign a global variable inside a function you have to *declare* the variable global before you use it:

```
been_called = false

function example2()
    global been_called
    been_called = true
end
```

The *global statement* tells the interpreter something like, "In this function, when I say been_called, I mean the global variable; don't create a local one."

Here's an example that tries to update a global variable:

```
counter = 0

function example3()
    counter = counter + 1          # WRONG
end
```

If you run it you get:

```
julia> example3()
ERROR: UndefVarError: count not defined
```

Julia assumes that count is local, and under that assumption you are reading it before writing it. The solution, again, is to declare count global:

```
count = 0

function example3()
    global counter
    counter += 1
end
```

If a global variable refers to a mutable value, you can modify the value without declaring the variable global:

```
known = Dict(0=>0, 1=>1)

function example4()
    known[2] = 1
end
```

So, you can add, remove, and replace elements of a global array or dictionary, but if you want to reassign the variable, you have to declare it global:

```
known = Dict(0=>0, 1=>1)

function example5()
    global known
    known = Dict()
end
```

For performance reasons, you should declare a global variable *constant*. You can no longer reassign the variable, but if it refers to a mutable value, you can modify the value:

```
const known = Dict(0=>0, 1=>1)

function example4()
    known[2] = 1
end
```

Global variables can be useful, but if you have a lot of them, and you modify them frequently, they can make programs hard to debug and perform badly.

Debugging

As you work with bigger datasets, it can become unwieldy to debug by printing and checking the output by hand. Here are some suggestions for debugging large datasets:

- Scale down the input.

  If possible, reduce the size of the dataset. For example, if the program reads a text file, start with just the first 10 lines, or with the smallest example you can find that errors. You should not edit the files themselves, but rather modify the program so it reads only the first n lines.

  If there is an error, you can reduce n to the smallest value that manifests the error, and then increase it gradually as you find and correct errors.

- Check summaries and types.

  Instead of printing and checking the entire dataset, consider printing summaries of the data: for example, the number of items in a dictionary or the total of an array of numbers.

  A common cause of runtime errors is a value that is not the right type. For debugging this kind of error, it is often enough to print the type of a value.

- Write self-checks.

  Sometimes you can write code to check for errors automatically. For example, if you are computing the average of an array of numbers, you could check that the result is not greater than the largest element in the array or less than the smallest. This is called a "sanity check."

  Another kind of check compares the results of two different computations to see if they are consistent. This is called a "consistency check."

- Format the output.

  Formatting debugging output can make it easier to spot an error. We saw an example in "Debugging" on page 73.

  Again, time you spend building scaffolding can reduce the time you spend debugging.

Glossary

dictionary
> A mapping from keys to their corresponding values.

key
> An object that appears in a dictionary as the first part of a key-value pair.

value
> An object that appears in a dictionary as the second part of a key-value pair. This is more specific than our previous use of the word "value."

key-value pair
> The representation of the mapping from a key to a value.

item
> In a dictionary, another name for a key-value pair.

mapping
> A relationship in which each element of one set corresponds to an element of another set.

hash table
> The algorithm used to implement Julia dictionaries.

implementation
> A way of performing a computation.

lookup
> A dictionary operation that takes a key and finds the corresponding value.

reverse lookup
> A dictionary operation that takes a value and finds one or more keys that map to it.

singleton
> An array (or other sequence) with a single element.

hashable
> A type that has a hash function.

hash function
> A function used by a hash table to compute the location for a key.

call graph
> A diagram that shows every frame created during the execution of a program, with an arrow from each caller to each callee.

memo
> A computed value stored to avoid unnecessary future computation.

global variable
> A variable defined outside a function. Global variables can be accessed from any function.

flag
> A Boolean variable used to indicate whether a condition is true.

declaration
> A statement like `global` that tells the interpreter something about a variable.

global statement
> A statement that declares a variable name global.

constant global variable
> A global variable that cannot be reassigned.

Exercises

Exercise 11-2

Write a function that reads the words in *words.txt* and stores them as keys in a dictionary. It doesn't matter what the values are. Then you can use the ∈ operator as a fast way to check whether a string is in the dictionary.

If you did "Exercise 10-10" on page 125, you can compare the speed of this implementation with the array ∈ operator and the bisection search.

Exercise 11-3

Read the documentation of the dictionary function `get!` and use it to write a more concise version of `invertdict`.

Exercise 11-4

Memoize the Ackermann function from "Exercise 6-5" on page 75 and see if memoization makes it possible to evaluate the function with bigger arguments.

Exercise 11-5

If you did "Exercise 10-7" on page 125, you already have a function named `hasduplicates` that takes an array as a parameter and returns `true` if there is any object that appears more than once in the array.

Use a dictionary to write a faster, simpler version of `hasduplicates`.

Exercise 11-6

Two words are "rotate pairs" if you can rotate one of them and get the other (see rotateword in "Exercise 8-11" on page 99).

Write a program that reads a word array and finds all the rotate pairs.

Exercise 11-7

Here's another Puzzler from *Car Talk* (*http://bit.ly/2OM2Fwp*):

> [A contributor] came upon a common one-syllable, five-letter word recently that has the following unique property. When you remove the first letter, the remaining letters form a homophone of the original word, that is a word that sounds exactly the same. Replace the first letter, that is, put it back and remove the second letter and the result is yet another homophone of the original word. And the question is, what's the word?

> Now I'm going to give you an example that doesn't work. Let's look at the five-letter word, 'wrack.' W-R-A-C-K, you know like to 'wrack with pain.' If I remove the first letter, I am left with a four-letter word, 'R-A-C-K.' As in, 'Holy cow, did you see the rack on that buck! It must have been a nine-pointer!' It's a perfect homophone. If you put the 'w' back, and remove the 'r,' instead, you're left with the word, 'wack,' which is a real word, it's just not a homophone of the other two words.

> But there is, however, at least one word that [I] know of, which will yield two homophones if you remove either of the first two letters to make two, new four-letter words. The question is, what's the word?

You can use the dictionary from "Exercise 11-2" on page 139 to check whether a string is in the word array.

 To check whether two words are homophones, you can use the Carnegie Mellon University Pronouncing Dictionary (*http://bit.ly/2IcBZmZ*).

Write a program that lists all the words that solve the Puzzler.

CHAPTER 12

Tuples

This chapter presents one more built-in type, the tuple, and then shows how arrays, dictionaries, and tuples work together. It also introduces a useful feature for variable-length argument arrays, the gather and scatter operators.

Tuples Are Immutable

A *tuple* is a sequence of values. The values can be of any type, and they are indexed by integers, so in that respect tuples are a lot like arrays. The important difference is that tuples are immutable and that each element can have its own type.

Syntactically, a tuple is a comma-separated list of values:

```
julia> t = 'a', 'b', 'c', 'd', 'e'
('a', 'b', 'c', 'd', 'e')
```

Although it is not necessary, it is common to enclose tuples in parentheses:

```
julia> t = ('a', 'b', 'c', 'd', 'e')
('a', 'b', 'c', 'd', 'e')
```

To create a tuple with a single element, you have to include a final comma:

```
julia> t1 = ('a',)
('a',)
julia> typeof(t1)
Tuple{Char}
```

 A value in parentheses without comma is not a tuple:

```
julia> t2 = ('a')
'a': ASCII/Unicode U+0061 (category Ll: Letter,
  lowercase)
julia> typeof(t2)
Char
```

Another way to create a tuple is using the built-in function `tuple`. With no argument, it creates an empty tuple:

```julia
julia> tuple()
()
```

If multiple arguments are provided, the result is a tuple with the given arguments:

```julia
julia> t3 = tuple(1, 'a', pi)
(1, 'a', π = 3.1415926535897...)
```

Because `tuple` is the name of a built-in function, you should avoid using it as a variable name.

Most array operators also work on tuples. The bracket operator indexes an element:

```julia
julia> t = ('a', 'b', 'c', 'd', 'e');

julia> t[1]
'a': ASCII/Unicode U+0061 (category Ll: Letter, lowercase)
```

And the slice operator selects a range of elements:

```julia
julia> t[2:4]
('b', 'c', 'd')
```

But if you try to modify one of the elements of the tuple, you get an error:

```julia
julia> t[1] = 'A'
ERROR: MethodError: no method matching setindex!(::NTuple{5,Char},
    ::Char, ::Int64)
```

Because tuples are immutable, you can't modify the elements.

The relational operators work with tuples and other sequences. Julia starts by comparing the first element from each sequence. If they are equal, it goes on to the next elements, and so on until it finds elements that differ. Subsequent elements are not considered (even if they are really big):

```julia
julia> (0, 1, 2) < (0, 3, 4)
true
julia> (0, 1, 2000000) < (0, 3, 4)
true
```

Tuple Assignment

It is often useful to swap the values of two variables. With conventional assignments, you have to use a temporary variable. For example, to swap a and b:

```julia
temp = a
a = b
b = temp
```

This solution is cumbersome; *tuple assignment* is more elegant:

```
a, b = b, a
```

The left side is a tuple of variables; the right side is a tuple of expressions. Each value is assigned to its respective variable. All the expressions on the right side are evaluated before any of the assignments.

The number of variables on the left has to be fewer than the number of values on the right:

```
julia> (a, b) = (1, 2, 3)
(1, 2, 3)
julia> a, b, c = 1, 2
ERROR: BoundsError: attempt to access (1, 2)
  at index [3]
```

More generally, the right side can be any kind of sequence (string, array, or tuple). For example, to split an email address into a username and a domain, you could write:

```
julia> addr = "julius.caesar@rome"
"julius.caesar@rome"
julia> uname, domain = split(addr, '@');
```

The return value from split is an array with two elements; the first element is assigned to uname, the second to domain:

```
julia> uname
"julius.caesar"
julia> domain
"rome"
```

Tuples as Return Values

Strictly speaking, a function can only return one value, but if the value is a tuple, the effect is the same as returning multiple values. For example, if you want to divide two integers and compute the quotient and remainder, it is inefficient to compute x ÷ y and then x % y. It is better to compute them both at the same time.

The built-in function divrem takes two arguments and returns a tuple of two values, the quotient and remainder. You can store the result as a tuple:

```
julia> t = divrem(7, 3)
(2, 1)
```

Or use tuple assignment to store the elements separately:

```
julia> q, r = divrem(7, 3);

julia> @show q r;
q = 2
r = 1
```

Here is an example of a function that returns a tuple:

```
function minmax(t)
    minimum(t), maximum(t)
end
```

`maximum` and `minimum` are built-in functions that find the largest and smallest elements of a sequence. `minmax` computes both and returns a tuple of two values. The built-in function `extrema` is more efficient.

Variable-Length Argument Tuples

Functions can take a variable number of arguments. A parameter name that ends with ... *gathers* arguments into a tuple. For example, `printall` takes any number of arguments and prints them:

```
function printall(args...)
    println(args)
end
```

The gather parameter can have any name you like, but `args` is conventional. Here's how the function works:

```
julia> printall(1, 2.0, '3')
(1, 2.0, '3')
```

The complement of gather is *scatter*. If you have a sequence of values and you want to pass it to a function as multiple arguments, you can use the ... operator. For example, `divrem` takes exactly two arguments; it doesn't work with a tuple:

```
julia> t = (7, 3);

julia> divrem(t)
ERROR: MethodError: no method matching divrem(::Tuple{Int64,Int64})
```

But if you scatter the tuple, it works:

```
julia> divrem(t...)
(2, 1)
```

Many of the built-in functions use variable-length argument tuples. For example, `max` and `min` can take any number of arguments:

```
julia> max(1, 2, 3)
3
```

But `sum` does not:

```
julia> sum(1, 2, 3)
ERROR: MethodError: no method matching sum(::Int64, ::Int64, ::Int64)
```

Exercise 12-1

Write a function called `sumall` that takes any number of arguments and returns their sum.

In the Julia world, gather is often called "slurp" and scatter "splat."

Arrays and Tuples

`zip` is a built-in function that takes two or more sequences and returns a collection of tuples where each tuple contains one element from each sequence. The name of the function refers to a zipper, which joins and interleaves two rows of teeth.

This example zips a string and an array:

```
julia> s = "abc";

julia> t = [1, 2, 3];

julia> zip(s, t)
Base.Iterators.Zip{Tuple{String,Array{Int64,1}}}(("abc", [1, 2, 3]))
```

The result is a *zip object* that knows how to iterate through the pairs. The most common use of `zip` is in a for loop:

```
julia> for pair in zip(s, t)
           println(pair)
       end
('a', 1)
('b', 2)
('c', 3)
```

A zip object is a kind of *iterator*, which is any object that iterates through a sequence. Iterators are similar to arrays in some ways, but unlike arrays, you can't use an index to select an element from an iterator.

If you want to use array operators and functions, you can use a zip object to make an array:

```
julia> collect(zip(s, t))
3-element Array{Tuple{Char,Int64},1}:
 ('a', 1)
 ('b', 2)
 ('c', 3)
```

The result is an array of tuples; in this example, each tuple contains a character from the string and the corresponding element from the array.

If the sequences are not the same length, the result has the length of the shorter one:

```
julia> collect(zip("Anne", "Elk"))
3-element Array{Tuple{Char,Char},1}:
```

```
('A', 'E')
('n', 'l')
('n', 'k')
```

You can use tuple assignment in a for loop to traverse an array of tuples:

```
julia> t = [('a', 1), ('b', 2), ('c', 3)];

julia> for (letter, number) in t
           println(number, " ", letter)
       end
1 a
2 b
3 c
```

Each time through the loop, Julia selects the next tuple in the array and assigns the elements to letter and number. The parentheses around (letter, number) are compulsory.

If you combine zip, for, and tuple assignment, you get a useful idiom for traversing two (or more) sequences at the same time. For example, hasmatch takes two sequences, t1 and t2, and returns true if there is an index i such that t1[i] == t2[i]:

```
function hasmatch(t1, t2)
    for (x, y) in zip(t1, t2)
        if x == y
            return true
        end
    end
    false
end
```

If you need to traverse the elements of a sequence and their indices, you can use the built-in function enumerate:

```
julia> for (index, element) in enumerate("abc")
           println(index, " ", element)
       end
1 a
2 b
3 c
```

The result from enumerate is an enumerate object, which iterates a sequence of pairs; each pair contains an index (starting from 1) and an element from the given sequence.

Dictionaries and Tuples

Dictionaries can be used as iterators that iterate the key-value pairs. You can use a dictionary in a for loop like this:

```
julia> d = Dict('a'=>1, 'b'=>2, 'c'=>3);

julia> for (key, value) in d
           println(key, " ", value)
       end
a 1
c 3
b 2
```

As you should expect from a dictionary, the items are in no particular order.

Going in the other direction, you can use an array of tuples to initialize a new dictionary:

```
julia> t = [('a', 1), ('c', 3), ('b', 2)];

julia> d = Dict(t)
Dict{Char,Int64} with 3 entries:
  'a' => 1
  'c' => 3
  'b' => 2
```

Combining `Dict` with `zip` yields a concise way to create a dictionary:

```
julia> d = Dict(zip("abc", 1:3))
Dict{Char,Int64} with 3 entries:
  'a' => 1
  'c' => 3
  'b' => 2
```

It is common to use tuples as keys in dictionaries. For example, a telephone directory might map from *last-name, first-name* pairs to telephone numbers. Assuming that we have defined `last`, `first`, and `number`, we could write:

```
directory[last, first] = number
```

The expression in brackets is a tuple. We could use tuple assignment to traverse this dictionary:

```
for ((last, first), number) in directory
    println(first, " ", last, " ", number)
end
```

This loop traverses the key-value pairs in `directory`, which are tuples. It assigns the elements of the key in each tuple to `last` and `first`, and the value to `number`, then prints the name and corresponding telephone number.

There are two ways to represent tuples in a state diagram. The more detailed version shows the indices and elements just as they appear in an array. For example, the tuple (`"Cleese"`, `"John"`) would appear as in Figure 12-1.

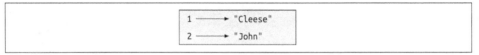

Figure 12-1. State diagram

But in a larger diagram you might want to leave out the details. For example, a diagram of the telephone directory might appear as in Figure 12-2.

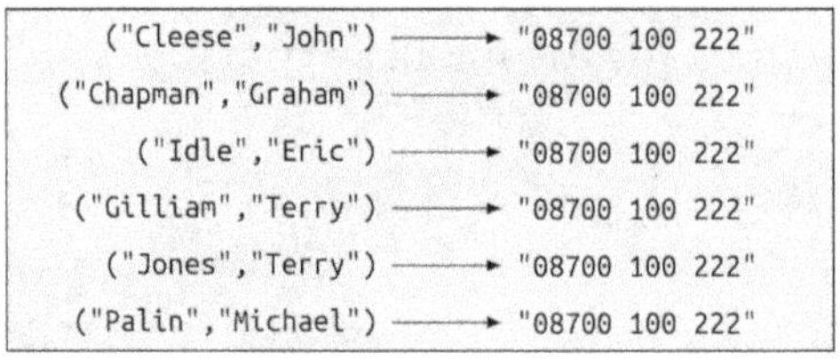

```
("Cleese","John")    ────▶ "08700 100 222"
("Chapman","Graham") ────▶ "08700 100 222"
("Idle","Eric")      ────▶ "08700 100 222"
("Gilliam","Terry")  ────▶ "08700 100 222"
("Jones","Terry")    ────▶ "08700 100 222"
("Palin","Michael")  ────▶ "08700 100 222"
```

Figure 12-2. State diagram

Here the tuples are shown using Julia syntax as a graphical shorthand. The telephone number in the diagram is the complaints line for the BBC, so please don't call it.

Sequences of Sequences

I have focused on arrays of tuples, but almost all of the examples in this chapter also work with arrays of arrays, tuples of tuples, and tuples of arrays. To avoid enumerating the possible combinations, it is sometimes easier to talk about sequences of sequences.

In many contexts, the different kinds of sequences (strings, arrays, and tuples) can be used interchangeably. So how should you choose one over the others?

To start with the obvious, strings are more limited than other sequences because the elements have to be characters. They are also immutable. If you need the ability to change the characters in a string (as opposed to creating a new string), you might want to use an array of characters instead.

Arrays are more common than tuples, mostly because they are mutable. But there are a few cases where you might prefer tuples:

- In some contexts, like a `return` statement, it is syntactically simpler to create a tuple than an array.
- If you are passing a sequence as an argument to a function, using tuples reduces the potential for unexpected behavior due to aliasing.
- For performance reasons. The compiler can specialize on the type.

Because tuples are immutable, they don't provide functions like `sort!` and `reverse!`, which modify existing arrays. But Julia provides the built-in functions `sort`, which takes an array and returns a new array with the same elements in sorted order, and `reverse`, which takes any sequence and returns a sequence of the same type in reverse order.

Debugging

Arrays, dictionaries, and tuples are examples of *data structures*; in this chapter we are starting to see compound data structures, like arrays of tuples, or dictionaries that contain tuples as keys and arrays as values. Compound data structures are useful, but they are prone to what I call *shape errors*; that is, errors caused when a data structure has the wrong type, size, or structure. For example, if you are expecting an array with one integer and I give you a plain old integer (not in an array), it won't work.

Julia allows you to attach a type to elements of a sequence. How this is done is detailed in Chapter 17. Specifying the type eliminates a lot of shape errors.

Glossary

tuple
> An immutable sequence of elements where every element can have its own type.

tuple assignment
> An assignment with a sequence on the right side and a tuple of variables on the left. The right side is evaluated and then its elements are assigned to the variables on the left.

gather
> The operation of assembling a variable-length argument tuple.

scatter
> The operation of treating a sequence as a list of arguments.

zip object
> The result of calling a built-in function `zip`, an object that iterates through a sequence of tuples.

iterator
> An object that can iterate through a sequence, but that does not provide array operators and functions.

data structure
> A collection of related values, often organized in arrays, dictionaries, tuples, etc.

shape error

An error caused because a value has the wrong shape; that is, the wrong type or size.

Exercises

Exercise 12-2

Write a function called `mostfrequent` that takes a string and prints the letters in decreasing order of frequency. Find text samples from several different languages and see how letter frequency varies between languages. Compare your results with the tables at *https://en.wikipedia.org/wiki/Letter_frequencies*.

Exercise 12-3

More anagrams!

1. Write a program that reads a word list from a file (see "Reading Word Lists" on page 101) and prints all the sets of words that are anagrams.

    Here is an example of what the output might look like:

    ```
    ["deltas", "desalt", "lasted", "salted", "slated", "staled"]
    ["retainers", "ternaries"]
    ["generating", "greatening"]
    ["resmelts", "smelters", "termless"]
    ```

     You might want to build a dictionary that maps from a collection of letters to an array of words that can be spelled with those letters. The question is, how can you represent the collection of letters in a way that can be used as a key?

2. Modify the previous program so that it prints the longest array of anagrams first, followed by the second longest, and so on.

3. In Scrabble a "bingo" is when you play all seven tiles in your rack, along with a letter on the board, to form an eight-letter word. What collection of eight letters forms the most possible bingos?

Exercise 12-4

Two words form a "metathesis pair" if you can transform one into the other by swapping two letters; for example, "converse" and "conserve." Write a program that finds all of the metathesis pairs in *words.txt*.

Don't test all pairs of words, and don't test all possible swaps.

Credit: This exercise is inspired by an example at *http://puzzlers.org*.

Exercise 12-5

Here's another *Car Talk* Puzzler (*http://bit.ly/2OM2Fwp*):

> What is the longest English word, that remains a valid English word, as you remove its letters one at a time?
>
> Now, letters can be removed from either end, or the middle, but you can't rearrange any of the letters. Every time you drop a letter, you wind up with another English word. If you do that, you're eventually going to wind up with one letter and that too is going to be an English word—one that's found in the dictionary. I want to know what's the longest word. What's the word, and how many letters does it have?
>
> I'm going to give you a little modest example: Sprite. Ok? You start off with sprite, you take a letter off, one from the interior of the word, take the r away, and we're left with the word spite, then we take the e off the end, we're left with spit, we take the s off, we're left with pit, it, and I.

Write a program to find all words that can be reduced in this way, and then find the longest one.

This exercise is a little more challenging than most, so here are some suggestions:

1. You might want to write a function that takes a word and computes an array of all the words that can be formed by removing one letter. These are the "children" of the word.

2. Recursively, a word is reducible if any of its children are reducible. As a base case, you can consider the empty string reducible.

3. The word list I provided, *words.txt*, doesn't contain single-letter words. So, you might want to add "I," "a," and the empty string.

4. To improve the performance of your program, you might want to memoize the words that are known to be reducible.

CHAPTER 13

Case Study: Data Structure Selection

At this point you have learned about Julia's core data structures, and you have seen some of the algorithms that use them.

This chapter presents a case study with exercises that let you think about choosing data structures and practice using them.

Word Frequency Analysis

As usual, you should at least attempt the exercises before you read my solutions.

Exercise 13-1

Write a program that reads a file, breaks each line into words, strips whitespace and punctuation from the words, and converts them to lowercase.

 The function isletter tests whether a character is alphabetic.

Exercise 13-2

Go to Project Gutenberg (*https://gutenberg.org*) and download your favorite out-of-copyright book in plain text format.

Modify your program from the previous exercise to read the book you downloaded, skip over the header information at the beginning of the file, and process the rest of the words as before.

Then modify the program to count the total number of words in the book, and the number of times each word is used.

Print the number of different words used in the book. Compare different books by different authors, written in different eras. Which author uses the most extensive vocabulary?

Exercise 13-3

Modify the program from the previous exercise to print the 20 most frequently used words in the book.

Exercise 13-4

Modify the previous program to read a word list and then print all the words in the book that are not in the word list. How many of them are typos? How many of them are common words that should be in the word list, and how many of them are really obscure?

Random Numbers

Given the same inputs, most computer programs generate the same outputs every time, so they are said to be *deterministic*. Determinism is usually a good thing, since we expect the same calculation to yield the same result. For some applications, though, we want the computer to be unpredictable. Games are an obvious example, but there are more.

Making a program truly nondeterministic turns out to be difficult, but there are ways to make it at least seem nondeterministic. One of them is to use algorithms that generate *pseudorandom* numbers. Pseudorandom numbers are not truly random because they are generated by a deterministic computation, but just by looking at the numbers it is all but impossible to distinguish them from random.

The function `rand` returns a random float between `0.0` and `1.0` (including `0.0` but not `1.0`). Each time you call `rand`, you get the next number in a long series. To see a sample, run this loop:

```
for i in 1:10
    x = rand()
    println(x)
end
```

The function `rand` can take an iterator or array as an argument and return a random element:

```
for i in 1:10
    x = rand(1:6)
```

```
        print(x, " ")
    end
```

Exercise 13-5

Write a function named choosefromhist that takes a histogram as defined in "Dictionaries as Collections of Counters" on page 129 and returns a random value from the histogram, chosen with probability in proportion to frequency. For example, for this histogram:

```
julia> t = ['a', 'a', 'b'];

julia> histogram(t)
Dict{Any,Any} with 2 entries:
  'a' => 2
  'b' => 1
```

your function should return 'a' with probability $\frac{2}{3}$ and 'b' with probability $\frac{1}{3}$.

Word Histogram

You should attempt the previous exercises before you go on. You will also need the *emma.txt* file available from this book's GitHub repository (*http://bit.ly/2TWQkpQ*).

Here is a program that reads a file and builds a histogram of the words in the file:

```
function processfile(filename)
    hist = Dict()
    for line in eachline(filename)
        processline(line, hist)
    end
    hist
end;

function processline(line, hist)
    line = replace(line, '-' => ' ')
    for word in split(line)
        word = string(filter(isletter, [word...])...)
        word = lowercase(word)
        hist[word] = get!(hist, word, 0) + 1
    end
end;

hist = processfile("emma.txt");
```

This program reads *emma.txt*, which contains the text of *Emma* by Jane Austen.

processfile loops through the lines of the file, passing them one at a time to processline. The histogram hist is being used as an accumulator.

`processline` uses the function `replace` to replace hyphens with spaces before using `split` to break the line into an array of strings. It traverses the array of words and uses `filter`, `isletter`, and `lowercase` to remove punctuation and convert to lower case. (It is shorthand to say that strings are "converted"; remember that strings are immutable, so a function like `lowercase` returns new strings.)

Finally, `processline` updates the histogram by creating a new item or incrementing an existing one.

To count the total number of words in the file, we can add up the frequencies in the histogram:

```
function totalwords(hist)
    sum(values(hist))
end
```

The number of different words is just the number of items in the dictionary:

```
function differentwords(hist)
    length(hist)
end
```

Here is some code to print the results:

```
julia> println("Total number of words: ", totalwords(hist))
Total number of words: 162742
julia> println("Number of different words: ", differentwords(hist))
Number of different words: 7380
```

Most Common Words

To find the most common words, we can make an array of tuples, where each tuple contains a word and its frequency, and sort it. The following function takes a histogram and returns an array of word-frequency tuples:

```
function mostcommon(hist)
    t = []
    for (key, value) in hist
        push!(t, (value, key))
    end
    reverse(sort(t))
end
```

In each tuple, the frequency appears first, so the resulting array is sorted by frequency. Here is a loop that prints the 10 most common words:

```
t = mostcommon(hist)
println("The most common words are:")
for (freq, word) in t[1:10]
    println(word, "\t", freq)
end
```

I use a tab character (`'\t'`) as a "separator," rather than a space, so the second column is lined up. Here are the results from *Emma*:

```
The most common words are:
to	5295
the	5266
and	4931
of	4339
i	3191
a	3155
it	2546
her	2483
was	2400
she	2364
```

 This code can be simplified using the `rev` keyword argument of the `sort` function. You can read about it in the documentation (*http://bit.ly/2CXCxdc*).

Optional Parameters

We have seen built-in functions that take optional arguments. It is possible to write programmer-defined functions with optional arguments, too. For example, here is a function that prints the most common words in a histogram:

```
function printmostcommon(hist, num=10)
    t = mostcommon(hist)
    println("The most common words are: ")
    for (freq, word) in t[1:num]
        println(word, "\t", freq)
    end
end
```

The first parameter is required; the second is optional. The *default value* of `num` is `10`.

If you only provide one argument:

```
printmostcommon(hist)
```

`num` gets the default value. If you provide two arguments:

```
printmostcommon(hist, 20)
```

`num` gets the value of the argument instead. In other words, the optional argument *overrides* the default value.

If a function has both required and optional parameters, all the required parameters have to come first, followed by the optional ones.

Dictionary Subtraction

Finding the words from a book that are not in the word list from *words.txt* is a problem you might recognize as set subtraction; that is, we want to find all the words from one set (the words in the book) that are not in the other (the words in the list).

`subtract` takes dictionaries d1 and d2 and returns a new dictionary that contains all the keys from d1 that are not in d2. Since we don't really care about the values, we set them all to `nothing`:

```
function subtract(d1, d2)
    res = Dict()
    for key in keys(d1)
        if key ∉ keys(d2)
            res[key] = nothing
        end
    end
    res
end
```

To find the words in the book you downloaded that are not in *words.txt*, you can use `processfile` to build a histogram for *words.txt*, and then `subtract`:

```
words = processfile("words.txt")
diff = subtract(hist, words)

println("Words in the book that aren't in the word list:")
for word in keys(diff)
    print(word, " ")
end
```

Here are some of the results from *Emma*:

```
Words in the book that aren't in the word list:
outree quicksighted outwardly adelaide rencontre jeffereys unreserved dixons
betweens ...
```

Some of these words are names and possessives. Others, like "rencontre," are no longer in common use. But a few are common words that should really be in the list!

Exercise 13-6

Julia provides a data structure called `Set` that provides many common set operations. You can read about them in "Collections and Data Structures" on page 238, or read the documentation (*http://bit.ly/2UgInAV*).

Write a program that uses set subtraction to find words in the book that are not in the word list.

Random Words

To choose a random word from the histogram, the simplest algorithm is to build an array with multiple copies of each word, according to the observed frequency, and then choose from the array:

```
function randomword(h)
    t = []
    for (word, freq) in h
        for i in 1:freq
            push!(t, word)
        end
    end
    rand(t)
end
```

This algorithm works, but it is not very efficient; each time you choose a random word it rebuilds the array, which is as big as the original book. An obvious improvement is to build the array once and then make multiple selections, but the array is still big.

An alternative is:

1. Use keys to get an array of the words in the book.

2. Build an array that contains the cumulative sum of the word frequencies (see "Exercise 10-2" on page 124). The last item in this array is the total number of words in the book, *n*.

3. Choose a random number from 1 to *n*. Use a bisection search (see "Exercise 10-10" on page 125) to find the index where the random number would be inserted in the cumulative sum.

4. Use the index to find the corresponding word in the word array.

Exercise 13-7

Write a program that uses this algorithm to choose a random word from the book.

Markov Analysis

If you choose words from the book at random, you can get a sense of the vocabulary, but you probably won't get a sentence:

```
this the small regard harriet which knightley's it most things
```

A series of random words seldom makes sense because there is no relationship between successive words. For example, in a real sentence you would expect an article like "the" to be followed by an adjective or a noun, and probably not a verb or adverb.

One way to measure these kinds of relationships is Markov analysis, which characterizes, for a given sequence of words, the probability of the words that might come next. For example, the song "Eric, the Half a Bee" (by Monty Python) begins:

Half a bee, philosophically,
Must, ipso facto, half not be.
But half the bee has got to be
Vis a vis, its entity. D'you see?

But can a bee be said to be
Or not to be an entire bee
When half the bee is not a bee
Due to some ancient injury?

In this text, the phrase "half the" is always followed by the word "bee," but the phrase "the bee" might be followed by either "has" or "is."

The result of Markov analysis is a mapping from each prefix (like "half the" and "the bee") to all possible suffixes (like "has" and "is").

Given this mapping, you can generate random text by starting with any prefix and choosing at random from the possible suffixes. Next, you can combine the end of the prefix and the new suffix to form the next prefix, and repeat.

For example, if you start with the prefix "Half a," then the next word has to be "bee," because the prefix only appears once in the text. The next prefix is "a bee," so the next suffix might be "philosophically," "be," or "due."

In this example the length of the prefix is always 2, but you can do Markov analysis with any prefix length.

Exercise 13-8

Give Markov analysis a try.

1. Write a program to read text from a file and perform Markov analysis. The result should be a dictionary that maps from prefixes to a collection of possible suffixes. The collection might be an array, tuple, or dictionary; it is up to you to make an appropriate choice. You can test your program with prefix length 2, but you should write the program in a way that makes it easy to try other lengths.

2. Add a function to the previous program to generate random text based on the Markov analysis. Here is an example from *Emma* with prefix length 2:

"He was very clever, be it sweetness or be angry, ashamed or only amused, at such a stroke. She had never thought of Hannah till you were never meant for me?" "I cannot make speeches, Emma:" he soon cut it all himself."

For this example, I left the punctuation attached to the words. The result is almost syntactically correct, but not quite. Semantically, it almost makes sense, but not quite.

What happens if you increase the prefix length? Does the random text make more sense?

3. Once your program is working, you might want to try a mash-up: if you combine text from two or more books, the random text you generate will blend the vocabulary and phrases from the sources in interesting ways.

Credit: This case study is based on an example from *The Practice of Programming* by Brian Kernighan and Rob Pike (Addison-Wesley).

 You should attempt this exercise before you go on.

Data Structures

Using Markov analysis to generate random text is fun, but there is also a point to this exercise: data structure selection. In completing the previous exercise, you had to choose:

- How to represent the prefixes
- How to represent the collection of possible suffixes
- How to represent the mapping from each prefix to the collection of possible suffixes

The last one is easy: a dictionary is the obvious choice for a mapping from keys to corresponding values.

For the prefixes, the most obvious options are a string, array of strings, or tuple of strings.

For the suffixes, one option is an array; another is a histogram (dictionary).

How should you choose? The first step is to think about the operations you will need to implement for each data structure. For the prefixes, you need to be able to remove words from the beginning and add to the end. For example, if the current prefix is "Half a," and the next word is "bee," you need to be able to form the next prefix, "a bee."

Your first choice might be an array, since it is easy to add and remove elements.

For the collection of suffixes, the operations you need to perform include adding a new suffix (or increasing the frequency of an existing one) and choosing a random suffix.

Adding a new suffix is equally easy for the array implementation or the histogram. Choosing a random element from an array is easy; choosing from a histogram is harder to do efficiently (see "Exercise 13-7" on page 159).

So far we have been talking mostly about ease of implementation, but there are other factors to consider in choosing data structures. One is runtime. Sometimes there is a theoretical reason to expect one data structure to be faster than another; for example, I mentioned that the in operator is faster for dictionaries than for arrays, at least when the number of elements is large.

But often you don't know ahead of time which implementation will be faster. One option is to implement both of them and see which is better. This approach is called *benchmarking*. A practical alternative is to choose the data structure that is easiest to implement, and then see if it is fast enough for the intended application. If so, there is no need to go on. If not, there are tools, like the Profile module, that can identify the places in a program that take the most time.

The other factor to consider is storage space. For example, using a histogram for the collection of suffixes might take less space because you only have to store each word once, no matter how many times it appears in the text. In some cases, saving space can also make your program run faster, and in the extreme, your program might not run at all if you run out of memory. But for many applications, space is a secondary consideration after runtime.

One final thought: in this discussion, I have implied that you should use one data structure for both analysis and generation. But since these are separate phases, it would also be possible to use one structure for analysis and then convert to another structure for generation. This would be a net win if the time saved during generation exceeded the time spent in conversion.

 The Julia package DataStructures (*http://bit.ly/2FTXzKx*) implements a variety of data structures that are tailored to specific problems, such as an ordered dictionary whose entries can be iterated over deterministically.

Debugging

When you are debugging a program, and especially if you are working on a hard bug, there are five things to try:

Reading

Examine your code, read it back to yourself, and check that it says what you meant to say.

Running

Experiment by making changes and running different versions. Often if you display the right thing at the right place in the program, the problem becomes obvious, but sometimes you have to build scaffolding.

Ruminating

Take some time to think! What kind of error is it: syntax, runtime, or semantic? What information can you get from the error messages, or from the output of the program? What kind of error could cause the problem you're seeing? What did you change last, before the problem appeared?

Rubberducking

If you explain the problem to someone else, you sometimes find the answer before you finish asking the question. Often you don't need the other person; you could just talk to a rubber duck. And that's the origin of the well-known strategy called *rubber duck debugging*. I'm not making this up! (*http://bit.ly/2WNPcH7*)

Retreating

At some point, the best thing to do is back off, undoing recent changes, until you get back to a program that works and that you understand. Then you can start rebuilding.

Beginning programmers sometimes get stuck on one of these activities and forget the others. Each activity comes with its own failure mode.

For example, reading your code might help if the problem is a typographical error, but not if the problem is a conceptual misunderstanding. If you don't understand what your program does, you can read it 100 times and never see the error, because the error is in your head.

Running experiments can help, especially if you run small, simple tests. But if you run experiments without thinking or reading your code, you might fall into a pattern I call "random walk programming," which is the process of making random changes until the program does the right thing. Needless to say, random walk programming can take a long time.

You have to take time to think. As I've said already, debugging is like an experimental science. You should have at least one hypothesis about what the problem is. If there are two or more possibilities, try to think of a test that would eliminate one of them.

But even the best debugging techniques will fail if there are too many errors, or if the code you are trying to fix is too big and complicated. Sometimes the best option is to retreat, simplifying the program until you get to something that works and that you understand.

Beginning programmers are often reluctant to retreat because they can't stand to delete a line of code (even if it's wrong). If it makes you feel better, copy your program into another file before you start stripping it down. Then you can copy the pieces back one at a time.

Finding a hard bug requires reading, running, ruminating, and sometimes retreating. If you get stuck on one of these activities, try the others.

Glossary

deterministic
> Pertaining to a program that does the same thing each time it runs, given the same inputs.

pseudorandom
> Pertaining to a sequence of numbers that appears to be random, but is generated by a deterministic program.

default value
> The value given to an optional parameter if no argument is provided.

override
> To replace a default value with an argument.

benchmarking
> The process of choosing between data structures by implementing alternatives and testing them on a sample of the possible inputs.

rubberducking
> Debugging by explaining your problem to an inanimate object such as a rubber duck. Articulating the problem can help you solve it, even if the rubber duck doesn't know Julia.

Exercises

Exercise 13-9

The "rank" of a word is its position in an array of words sorted by frequency: the most common word has rank 1, the second most common has rank 2, etc.

Zipf's law (*http://bit.ly/2uKohQr*) describes a relationship between the ranks and frequencies of words in natural languages. Specifically, it predicts that the frequency, f, of the word with rank r is:

$$f = cr^{-s}$$

where s and c are parameters that depend on the language and the text. If you take the logarithm of both sides of this equation, you get:

$$\log f = \log c - s \log r$$

So if you plot $\log f$ versus $\log r$, you should get a straight line with slope $-s$ and intercept $\log c$.

Write a program that reads a text from a file, counts word frequencies, and prints one line for each word, in descending order of frequency, with $\log f$ and $\log r$.

Install a plotting library:

```
(v1.0) pkg> add Plots
```

Its usage is very easy:

```
using Plots
x = 1:10
y = x.^2
plot(x, y)
```

Use the Plots library to plot the results and check whether they form a straight line.

CHAPTER 14

Files

This chapter introduces the idea of persistent programs that keep data in permanent storage, and shows how to use different kinds of permanent storage, like files and databases.

Persistence

Most of the programs we have seen so far are transient, in the sense that they run for a short time and produce some output, but when they end, their data disappears. If you run the program again, it starts with a clean slate.

Other programs are *persistent*: they run for a long time (or all the time); they keep at least some of their data in permanent storage (a hard drive, for example); and if they shut down and restart, they pick up where they left off.

Examples of persistent programs are operating systems, which run pretty much whenever a computer is on, and web servers, which run all the time, waiting for requests to come in on the network.

One of the simplest ways for programs to maintain their data is by reading and writing text files. We have already seen programs that read text files; in this chapter we will see programs that write them.

An alternative is to store the state of the program in a database. In this chapter I will also present how to use a simple database.

Reading and Writing

A *text file* is a sequence of characters stored on a permanent medium like a hard drive or flash memory. We saw how to open and read a file in "Reading Word Lists" on page 101.

To write a file, you have to open it with mode "w" as a second parameter:

```
julia> fout = open("output.txt", "w")
IOStream(<file output.txt>)
```

If the file already exists, opening it in write mode clears out the old data and starts fresh, so be careful! If the file doesn't exist, a new one is created. open returns a file object and the write function puts data into the file:

```
julia> line1 = "This here's the wattle,\n";

julia> write(fout, line1)
24
```

The return value is the number of characters that were written. The file object keeps track of where it is, so if you call write again, it adds the new data to the end of the file:

```
julia> line2 = "the emblem of our land.\n";

julia> write(fout, line2)
24
```

When you are done writing, you should close the file:

```
julia> close(fout)
```

If you don't close the file, it gets closed for you when the program ends.

Formatting

The argument of *write* has to be a string, so if we want to put other values in a file, we have to convert them to strings. The easiest way to do that is with string or string interpolation:

```
julia> fout = open("output.txt", "w")
IOStream(<file output.txt>)
julia> write(fout, string(150))
3
```

An alternative is to use the print or print(ln) functions:

```
julia> camels = 42
42
julia> println(fout, "I have spotted $camels camels.")
```

A more powerful alternative is the @printf (*http://bit.ly/2HVLuYJ*) macro, which prints using a C-style format specification string.

Filenames and Paths

Files are organized into *directories* (also called "folders"). Every running program has a "current directory," which is the default directory for most operations. For example, when you open a file for reading, Julia looks for it in the current directory.

The function pwd returns the name of the current directory:

```
julia> cwd = pwd()
"/home/ben"
```

cwd stands for "current working directory." The result in this example is */home/ben*, which is the home directory of a user named *ben*.

A string like "/home/ben" that identifies a file or directory is called a *path*.

A simple filename like *memo.txt* is also considered a path, but it is a *relative path* because it relates to the current directory. If the current directory is */home/ben*, the filename *memo.txt* would refer to */home/ben/memo.txt*.

A path that begins with / does not depend on the current directory; it is called an *absolute path*. To find the absolute path to a file, you can use abspath:

```
julia> abspath("memo.txt")
"/home/ben/memo.txt"
```

Julia provides other functions for working with filenames and paths. For example, ispath checks whether a file or directory exists:

```
julia> ispath("memo.txt")
true
```

If it exists, isdir checks whether it's a directory:

```
julia> isdir("memo.txt")
false
julia> isdir("/home/ben")
true
```

Similarly, isfile checks whether it's a file.

readdir returns an array of the files (and other directories) in the given directory:

```
julia> readdir(cwd)
3-element Array{String,1}:
  "memo.txt"
```

```
    "music"
    "photos"
```

To demonstrate these functions, the following example "walks" through a directory, prints the names of all the files, and calls itself recursively on all the directories:

```
function walk(dirname)
    for name in readdir(dirname)
        path = joinpath(dirname, name)
        if isfile(path)
            println(path)
        else
            walk(path)
        end
    end
end
```

joinpath takes a directory and a filename and joins them into a complete path.

Julia provides a function called walkdir (*http://bit.ly/2Uj29fl*) that is similar to this one but more versatile. As an exercise, read the documentation and use it to print the names of the files in a given directory and its subdirectories.

Catching Exceptions

A lot of things can go wrong when you try to read and write files. If you try to open a file that doesn't exist, you get a SystemError:

```
julia> fin = open("bad_file")
ERROR: SystemError: opening file "bad_file": No such file or directory
```

The same thing happens if you don't have permission to access a file:

```
julia> fout = open("/etc/passwd", "w")
ERROR: SystemError: opening file "/etc/passwd": Permission denied
```

To avoid these errors you could use functions like ispath and isfile, but it would take a lot of time and code to check all the possibilities.

It's easier to go ahead and try, and deal with problems if they happen—which is exactly what the try statement does. The syntax is similar to an if statement:

```
try
    fin = open("bad_file.txt")
catch exc
    println("Something went wrong: $exc")
end
```

Julia starts by executing the `try` clause. If all goes well, it skips the `catch` clause and proceeds. If an exception occurs, it jumps out of the `try` clause and runs the `catch` clause.

Handling an exception with a `try` statement is called *catching* an exception. In this example, the `except` clause prints an error message that is not very helpful. In general, catching an exception gives you a chance to fix the problem, or try again, or at least end the program gracefully.

In code that performs state changes or uses resources like files, there is typically cleanup work (such as closing files) that needs to be done when the code is finished. Exceptions potentially complicate this task, since they can cause a block of code to exit before reaching its normal end. The `finally` keyword provides a way to run some code when a given block of code exits, regardless of how it exits:

```
f = open("output.txt")
try
    line = readline(f)
    println(line)
finally
    close(f)
end
```

The function `close` will always be executed.

Databases

A *database* is a file that is organized for storing data. Many databases are organized like dictionaries, in the sense that they map from keys to values. The biggest difference between a database and a dictionary is that the database is on disk (or other permanent storage), so it persists after the program ends.

ThinkJulia provides an interface to the GDBM (GNU dbm) library of functions for creating and updating database files. As an example, I'll create a database that contains captions for image files.

Opening a database is similar to opening other files:

```
julia> using ThinkJulia

julia> db = DBM("captions", "c")
DBM(<captions>)
```

The mode `"c"` means that the database should be created if it doesn't already exist. The result is a database object that can be used (for most operations) like a dictionary.

When you create a new item, GDBM updates the database file:

```
julia> db["cleese.png"] = "Photo of John Cleese."
"Photo of John Cleese."
```

When you access one of the items, GDBM reads the file:

```julia
julia> db["cleese.png"]
"Photo of John Cleese."
```

If you make another assignment to an existing key, GDBM replaces the old value:

```julia
julia> db["cleese.png"] = "Photo of John Cleese doing a silly walk."
"Photo of John Cleese doing a silly walk."
julia> db["cleese.png"]
"Photo of John Cleese doing a silly walk."
```

Some functions that take a dictionary as an argument, like keys and values, don't work with database objects. But iteration with a for loop works:

```julia
for (key, value) in db
    println(key, ": ", value)
end
```

As with other files, you should close the database when you are done:

```julia
julia> close(db)
```

Serialization

A limitation of GDBM is that the keys and the values have to be strings or byte arrays. If you try to use any other type, you get an error.

The functions serialize and deserialize can help. The serialize function can translate almost any type of object into a byte array (an IOBuffer) suitable for storage in a database:

```julia
julia> using Serialization

julia> io = IOBuffer();

julia> t = [1, 2, 3];

julia> serialize(io, t)
24
julia> print(take!(io))
UInt8[0x37, 0x4a, 0x4c, 0x07, 0x04, 0x00, 0x00, 0x00, 0x15, 0x00, 0x08, 0xe2,
0x01, 0x00, 0x00, 0x00, 0x00, 0x00, 0x00, 0x00, 0x02, 0x00, 0x00, 0x00, 0x00,
0x00, 0x00, 0x00, 0x03, 0x00, 0x00, 0x00, 0x00, 0x00, 0x00, 0x00]
```

The format isn't obvious to human readers; it is meant to be easy for Julia to interpret. deserialize reconstitutes the object:

```julia
julia> io = IOBuffer();

julia> t1 = [1, 2, 3];

julia> serialize(io, t1)
```

```
24
julia> s = take!(io);

julia> t2 = deserialize(IOBuffer(s));

julia> print(t2)
[1, 2, 3]
```

`serialize` and `deserialize` write to and read from an `IOBuffer` object that represents an in-memory I/O stream. The function `take!` fetches the contents of the `IOBuffer` as a byte array and resets the `IOBuffer` to its initial state.

Although the new object has the same value as the old one, it is not (in general) the same object:

```
julia> t1 == t2
true
julia> t1 ≡ t2
false
```

In other words, serialization and then deserialization has the same effect as copying the object.

You can use this to store nonstrings in a database.

In fact, the storage of nonstrings in a database is so common that this functionality has been encapsulated in a package called JLD2 (*http://bit.ly/2TRWJCU*).

Command Objects

Most operating systems provide a command-line interface, also known as a *shell*. Shells usually provide commands to navigate the filesystem and launch applications. For example, in Unix you can change directories with `cd`, display the contents of a directory with `ls`, and launch a web browser by typing (for example) `firefox`.

Any program that you can launch from the shell can also be launched from Julia using a *command object*:

```
julia> cmd = `echo hello`
`echo hello`
```

Backticks are used to delimit the command.

The function `run` executes the command:

```
julia> run(cmd);
hello
```

hello is the output of the echo command, sent to STDOUT. The run function itself returns a process object, and throws an ErrorException if the external command fails to run successfully.

If you want to read the output of the external command, read can be used instead:

```
julia> a = read(cmd, String)
"hello\n"
```

For example, most Unix systems provide a command called md5sum or md5 that reads the contents of a file and computes an MD5 checksum (*http://bit.ly/2G2nhxx*). This command provides an efficient way to check whether two files have the same contents. The probability that different contents will yield the same checksum is very small (i.e., unlikely to happen before the universe collapses).

You can use a command object to run md5 from Julia and get the result:

```
julia> filename = "output.txt"
"output.txt"
julia> cmd = `md5 $filename`
`md5 output.txt`
julia> res = read(cmd, String)
"MD5 (output.txt) = d41d8cd98f00b204e9800998ecf8427e\n"
```

Modules

Suppose you have a file named *wc.jl* with the following code:

```
function linecount(filename)
    count = 0
    for line in eachline(filename)
        count += 1
    end
    count
end

print(linecount("wc.jl"))
```

If you run this program, it reads itself and prints the number of lines in the file, which is 9. You can also include it in the REPL like this:

```
julia> include("wc.jl")
9
```

What if you don't want the linecount function to be directly available in Main, but you'd still like to use the function in different parts of your code? Julia introduces *modules* to create separate variable workspaces.

A module starts with the keyword module and ends with end. Using modules allows you to avoid naming conflicts between your own top-level definitions and those found in somebody else's code. import allows you to control which names from other modules are visible, and export specifies which of your names are public (i.e., can be used outside the module without being prefixed with the name of the module):

```
module LineCount
    export linecount

    function linecount(filename)
        count = 0
        for line in eachline(filename)
            count += 1
        end
        count
    end
end
```

The using statement allows you to make use of a module's public names from elsewhere, so you can use the linecount function that LineCount provides outside that module as follows:

```
julia> using LineCount

julia> linecount("wc.jl")
11
```

Exercise 14-1

Type this example into a file named *wc.jl*, include it into the REPL, and enter **using LineCount**.

If you import a module that has already been imported, Julia does nothing. It does not reread the file, even if it has changed.

If you want to reload a module, you have to restart the REPL. If you want to avoid this, you can use the Revise (*http://bit.ly/ 2uLW2Ru*) package to keep your sessions running longer.

Debugging

When you are reading and writing files, you might run into problems with whitespace. These errors can be hard to debug because spaces, tabs, and newlines are normally invisible:

```
julia> s = "1 2\t 3\n 4";

julia> println(s)
1 2	 3
 4
```

The built-in functions repr and dump can help. They take any object as an argument and return a string representation of the object:

```
julia> repr(s)
"\"1 2\\t 3\\n 4\""
julia> dump(s)
String "1 2\t 3\n 4"
```

This can be helpful for debugging.

One other problem you might run into is that different systems use different characters to indicate the end of a line. Some systems use a newline, represented by \n. Others use a Return character, represented by \r. Some use both. If you move files between different systems, these inconsistencies can cause problems.

For most systems, there are applications to convert from one format to another. You can read more about newline characters and conversion applications (*http://bit.ly/ 2Uj3nXZ*) or, of course, you could write one yourself.

Glossary

persistent
>   Pertaining to a program that runs indefinitely and keeps at least some of its data in permanent storage.

text file
>   A sequence of characters stored in permanent storage, like a hard drive.

directory
>   A named collection of files, also called a *folder*.

path
>   A string that identifies a file.

relative path
>   A path that starts from the current directory.

absolute path
>   A path that starts from the topmost directory in the filesystem.

catch
>   To prevent an exception from terminating a program using the try ... catch ... finally statements.

database
>   A file whose contents are organized like a dictionary with keys that correspond to values.

shell
>   A program that allows users to type commands and then executes them by starting other programs.

command object

An object that represents a shell command, allowing a Julia program to run commands and read the results.

module

A separate global variable workspace used to avoid naming conflicts.

Exercises

Exercise 14-2

Write a function called sed that takes as arguments a pattern string, a replacement string, and two filenames; it should read the first file and write the contents into the second file (creating it if necessary). If the pattern string appears anywhere in the file, it should be replaced with the replacement string.

If an error occurs while opening, reading, writing, or closing files, your program should catch the exception, print an error message, and exit.

Exercise 14-3

If you have done "Exercise 12-3" on page 150, you'll see that a dictionary is created that maps from a sorted string of letters to the array of words that can be spelled with those letters. For example, "opst" maps to the array ["opts", "post", "pots", "spot", "stop", "tops"].

Write a module that imports anagramsets and provides two new functions: storeanagrams should store the anagram dictionary using JLD2, and readanagrams should look up a word and return an array of its anagrams.

Exercise 14-4

In a large collection of MP3 files, there may be more than one copy of the same song, stored in different directories or with different filenames. The goal of this exercise is to search for duplicates.

1. Write a program that searches a directory and all of its subdirectories, recursively, and returns an array of complete paths for all files with a given suffix (like *.mp3*).

2. To recognize duplicates, you can use md5sum or md5 to compute a "checksum" for each file. If two files have the same checksum, they probably have the same contents.

3. To double-check, you can use the Unix command diff.

CHAPTER 15

Structs and Objects

At this point you know how to use functions to organize code and built-in types to organize data. The next step is to learn how to build your own types to organize both code and data. This is a big topic; it will take a few chapters to get there.

Composite Types

We have used many of Julia's built-in types; now we are going to define a new type. As an example, we will create a type called `Point` that represents a point in two-dimensional space.

In mathematical notation, points are often written in parentheses with a comma separating the coordinates. For example, $(0, 0)$ represents the origin, and (x, y) represents the point x units to the right and y units up from the origin.

There are several ways we might represent points in Julia:

- We could store the coordinates separately in two variables, x and y.
- We could store the coordinates as elements in an array or tuple.
- We could create a new type to represent points as objects.

Creating a new type is more complicated than the other options, but it has advantages that will be apparent soon.

A programmer-defined *composite type* is also called a *struct*. The `struct` definition for a point looks like this:

```
struct Point
    x
    y
end
```

The header indicates that the new struct is called `Point`. The body defines the *attributes* or *fields* of the struct. The `Point` struct has two fields: x and y.

A struct is like a factory for creating objects. To create a point, you call `Point` as if it were a function having as arguments the values of the fields. When `Point` is used as a function, it is called a *constructor*:

```julia
julia> p = Point(3.0, 4.0)
Point(3.0, 4.0)
```

The return value is a reference to a `Point` object, which we assign to p.

Creating a new object is called *instantiation*, and the object is an *instance* of the type.

When you print an instance, Julia tells you what type it belongs to and what the values of the attributes are.

Every object is an instance of some type, so "object" and "instance" are interchangeable. But in this chapter I use "instance" to indicate that I am talking about a programmer-defined type.

A state diagram that shows an object and its fields is called an *object diagram*; see Figure 15-1.

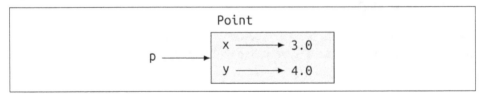

Figure 15-1. Object diagram

Structs Are Immutable

You can get the values of the fields using . notation:

```julia
julia> x = p.x
3.0
julia> p.y
4.0
```

The expression p.x means, "Go to the object p refers to and get the value of x." In the example, we assign that value to a variable named x. There is no conflict between the variable x and the field x.

You can use dot notation as part of any expression. For example:

```julia
julia> distance = sqrt(p.x^2 + p.y^2)
5.0
```

Structs are, however, by default immutable; after construction the fields cannot change value:

```
julia> p.y = 1.0
ERROR: setfield! immutable struct of type Point cannot be changed
```

This may seem odd at first, but it has several advantages:

- It can be more efficient.
- It is not possible to violate the invariants provided by the type's constructors (see "Constructors" on page 200).
- Code using immutable objects can be easier to reason about.

Mutable Structs

Where required, mutable composite types can be declared with the keyword `mutable struct`. Here is the definition of a mutable point:

```
mutable struct MPoint
    x
    y
end
```

You can assign values to an instance of a mutable struct using dot notation:

```
julia> blank = MPoint(0.0, 0.0)
MPoint(0.0, 0.0)
julia> blank.x = 3.0
3.0
julia> blank.y = 4.0
4.0
```

Rectangles

Sometimes it is obvious what the fields of an object should be, but other times you have to make decisions. For example, imagine you are designing a type to represent rectangles. What fields would you use to specify the location and size of a rectangle? You can ignore angle; to keep things simple, assume that the rectangle is either vertical or horizontal.

There are at least two possibilities:

- You could specify one corner of the rectangle (or the center), the width, and the height.
- You could specify two opposing corners.

At this point it is hard to say whether one is better than the other, so we'll implement the first one, just as an example:

```
"""
Represents a rectangle.

fields: width, height, corner
"""
struct Rectangle
    width
    height
    corner
end
```

The docstring lists the fields: `width` and `height` are numbers; `corner` is a `Point` object that specifies the lower-left corner.

To represent a rectangle, you have to instantiate a `Rectangle` object:

```
julia> origin = MPoint(0.0, 0.0)
MPoint(0.0, 0.0)
julia> box = Rectangle(100.0, 200.0, origin)
Rectangle(100.0, 200.0, MPoint(0.0, 0.0))
```

Figure 15-2 shows the state of this object. An object that is a field of another object is *embedded*. Because the `corner` attribute refers to a mutable object, the latter is drawn outside the `Rectangle` object.

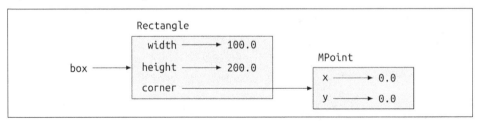

Figure 15-2. Object diagram

Instances as Arguments

You can pass an instance as an argument in the usual way. For example:

```
function printpoint(p)
    println("($(p.x), $(p.y))")
end
```

`printpoint` takes a `Point` as an argument and displays it in mathematical notation. To invoke it, you can pass p as an argument:

```
julia> printpoint(blank)
(3.0, 4.0)
```

Exercise 15-1

Write a function called `distancebetweenpoints` that takes two points as arguments and returns the distance between them.

If a mutable struct object is passed to a function as an argument, the function can modify the fields of the object. For example, `movepoint!` takes a mutable `Point` object and two numbers, dx and dy, and adds the numbers to, respectively, the x and the y attribute of the `Point`:

```
function movepoint!(p, dx, dy)
    p.x += dx
    p.y += dy
    nothing
end
```

Here is an example that demonstrates the effect:

```
julia> origin = MPoint(0.0, 0.0)
MPoint(0.0, 0.0)
julia> movepoint!(origin, 1.0, 2.0)

julia> origin
MPoint(1.0, 2.0)
```

Inside the function, p is an alias for `origin`, so when the function modifies p, `origin` changes.

Passing an immutable `Point` object to `movepoint!` causes an error:

```
julia> movepoint!(p, 1.0, 2.0)
ERROR: setfield! immutable struct of type Point cannot be changed
```

You can, however, modify the value of a mutable attribute of an immutable object. For example, `moverectangle!` has as arguments a `Rectangle` object and two numbers, dx and dy, and uses `movepoint!` to move the corner of the rectangle:

```
function moverectangle!(rect, dx, dy)
  movepoint!(rect.corner, dx, dy)
end
```

Now p in `movepoint!` is an alias for `rect.corner`, so when p is modified, `rect.corner` changes also:

```
julia> box
Rectangle(100.0, 200.0, MPoint(0.0, 0.0))
julia> moverectangle!(box, 1.0, 2.0)

julia> box
Rectangle(100.0, 200.0, MPoint(1.0, 2.0))
```

You cannot reassign a mutable attribute of an immutable object:

```
julia> box.corner = MPoint(1.0, 2.0)
ERROR: setfield! immutable struct of type Rectangle
    cannot be changed
```

Instances as Return Values

Functions can return instances. For example, `findcenter` takes a `Rectangle` as an argument and returns a `Point` that contains the coordinates of the center of the rectangle:

```
function findcenter(rect)
    Point(rect.corner.x + rect.width / 2, rect.corner.y + rect.height / 2)
end
```

The expression `rect.corner.x` means, "Go to the object `rect` refers to and select the field named `corner`; then go to that object and select the field named x."

Here is an example that passes box as an argument and assigns the resulting `Point` to center:

```
julia> center = findcenter(box)
Point(51.0, 102.0)
```

Copying

Aliasing can make a program difficult to read because changes in one place might have unexpected effects in another place. It is hard to keep track of all the variables that might refer to a given object.

Copying an object is often an alternative to aliasing. Julia provides a function called `deepcopy` that performs a *deep copy* and can duplicate any object, including the contents of any embedded objects:

```
julia> p1 = MPoint(3.0, 4.0)
MPoint(3.0, 4.0)
julia> p2 = deepcopy(p1)
MPoint(3.0, 4.0)
julia> p1 ≡ p2
false
julia> p1 == p2
false
```

The ≡ operator indicates that `p1` and `p2` are not the same object, which is what we expected. But you might have expected == to yield `true` because these points contain the same data. In that case, you will be disappointed to learn that for mutable objects, the default behavior of the == operator is the same as the === operator; it checks object identity, not object equivalence (see "Objects and Values" on page 117). That's because for mutable composite types, Julia doesn't know what should be considered equivalent—at least, not yet.

Exercise 15-2

Create a `Point` instance, make a copy of it, and check the equivalence and the egality of the two objects. The result may surprise you, but it explains why aliasing is a non-issue for an immutable object.

Debugging

When you start working with objects, you are likely to encounter some new exceptions. If you try to access a field that doesn't exist, you get:

```
julia> p = Point(3.0, 4.0)
Point(3.0, 4.0)
julia> p.z = 1.0
ERROR: type Point has no field z
Stacktrace:
 [1] setproperty!(::Point, ::Symbol, ::Float64) at ./sysimg.jl:19
 [2] top-level scope at none:0
```

If you are not sure what type an object is, you can ask:

```
julia> typeof(p)
Point
```

You can also use `isa` to check whether an object is an instance of a type:

```
julia> p isa Point
true
```

If you are not sure whether an object has a particular attribute, you can use the built-in function `fieldnames`:

```
julia> fieldnames(Point)
(:x, :y)
```

or the function `isdefined`:

```
julia> isdefined(p, :x)
true
julia> isdefined(p, :z)
false
```

The first argument can be any object; the second argument is a symbol, `:`, followed by the name of the field.

Glossary

struct

A user-defined type consisting of a collection of named fields. Also called a *composite type*.

attribute

One of the named values associated with an object. Also called a *field*.

constructor

A function with the same name as a type that creates instances of the type.

instantiate

To create a new object.

instance

An object that belongs to a certain type.

object diagram

A diagram that shows objects, their fields, and the values of the fields.

embedded object

An object that is stored as a field of another object.

deep copy

To copy the contents of an object as well as any embedded objects, and any objects embedded in them, and so on; implemented by the deepcopy function.

Exercises

Exercise 15-3

1. Write a definition for a type named Circle with fields center and radius, where center is a Point object and radius is a number.

2. Instantiate a Circle object that represents a circle with its center at (150, 100) and radius 75.

3. Write a function named pointincircle that takes a Circle object and a Point object and returns true if the point lies in or on the boundary of the circle.

4. Write a function named rectincircle that takes a Circle object and a Rectangle object and returns true if the rectangle lies entirely in or on the boundary of the circle.

5. Write a function named rectcircleoverlap that takes a Circle object and a Rectangle object and returns true if any of the corners of the rectangle fall

inside the circle. Or, as a more challenging version, return `true` if any part of the rectangle falls inside the circle.

Exercise 15-4

1. Write a function called `drawrect` that takes a `Turtle` object and a `Rectangle` object and uses the turtle to draw the rectangle. See Chapter 4 for examples using `Turtle` objects.

2. Write a function called `drawcircle` that takes a `Turtle` object and a `Circle` object and draws the circle.

Structs and Functions

Now that we know how to create new composite types, the next step is to write functions that take programmer-defined objects as parameters and return them as results. In this chapter I also present the "functional programming style" and two new program development plans.

Time

As another example of a composite type, we'll define a struct called `MyTime` that records the time of day. The struct definition looks like this:

```
"""
Represents the time of day.

fields: hour, minute, second
"""
struct MyTime
    hour
    minute
    second
end
```

The name `Time` is already used in Julia, so I've chosen this name to avoid a name clash. We can create a new `MyTime` object as follows:

```
julia> time = MyTime(11, 59, 30)
MyTime(11, 59, 30)
```

The object diagram for the `MyTime` object looks like Figure 16-1.

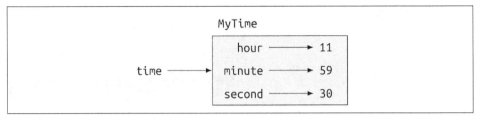

Figure 16-1. Object diagram

Exercise 16-1

Write a function called `printtime` that takes a `MyTime` object and prints it in the form `hour:minute:second`. The `@printf` macro of the standard library module `Printf` prints an integer with the format sequence `"%02d"` using at least two digits, including a leading zero if necessary.

Exercise 16-2

Write a Boolean function called `isafter` that takes two `MyTime` objects, `t1` and `t2`, and returns `true` if `t1` follows `t2` chronologically and `false` otherwise. Challenge: don't use an `if` statement.

Pure Functions

In the next few sections, we'll write two functions that add time values. They demonstrate two kinds of functions: pure functions and modifiers. They also demonstrate a development plan I'll call *prototype and patch*, which is a way of tackling a complex problem by starting with a simple prototype and incrementally dealing with the complications.

Here is a simple prototype of `addtime`:

```
function addtime(t1, t2)
    MyTime(t1.hour + t2.hour, t1.minute + t2.minute, t1.second + t2.second)
end
```

The function creates a new `MyTime` object, initializes its fields, and returns a reference to the new object. This is called a *pure function* because it does not modify any of the objects passed to it as arguments and it has no effect, like displaying a value or getting user input, other than returning a value.

To test this function, I'll create two `MyTime` objects: `start` contains the start time of a movie, like *Monty Python and the Holy Grail*, and `duration` contains the running time of the movie, which in this case is 1 hour 35 minutes.

`addtime` figures out when the movie will be done:

```
julia> start = MyTime(9, 45, 0);

julia> duration = MyTime(1, 35, 0);

julia> done = addtime(start, duration);

julia> printtime(done)
10:80:00
```

The result, `10:80:00`, might not be what you were hoping for. The problem is that this function does not deal with cases where the number of seconds or minutes adds up to more than 60. When that happens, we have to "carry" the extra seconds into the minute column or the extra minutes into the hour column. Here's an improved version:

```
function addtime(t1, t2)
    second = t1.second + t2.second
    minute = t1.minute + t2.minute
    hour = t1.hour + t2.hour
    if second >= 60
        second -= 60
        minute += 1
    end
    if minute >= 60
        minute -= 60
        hour += 1
    end
    MyTime(hour, minute, second)
end
```

Although this function is correct, it is starting to get big. We will see a shorter alternative later.

Modifiers

Sometimes it is useful for a function to modify the objects it gets as parameters. In that case, the changes are visible to the caller. Functions that work this way are called *modifiers*.

`increment!`, which adds a given number of seconds to a mutable `MyTime` object, can be written naturally as a modifier. Here is a rough draft:

```
function increment!(time, seconds)
    time.second += seconds
    if time.second >= 60
        time.second -= 60
        time.minute += 1
    end
    if time.minute >= 60
        time.minute -= 60
        time.hour += 1
```

```
        end
    end
```

The first line performs the basic operation; the remainder deals with the special cases we saw before.

Is this function correct? What happens if `seconds` is much greater than 60?

In that case, it is not enough to carry once; we have to keep doing it until `time.second` is less than 60. One solution is to replace the `if` statements with `while` statements. That would make the function correct, but not very efficient.

Exercise 16-3

Write a correct version of `increment!` that doesn't contain any loops.

Anything that can be done with modifiers can also be done with pure functions. In fact, some programming languages only allow pure functions. There is some evidence that programs that use pure functions are faster to develop and less error-prone than programs that use modifiers. But modifiers are convenient at times, and functional programs tend to be less efficient.

In general, I recommend that you write pure functions whenever it is reasonable and resort to modifiers only if there is a compelling advantage. This approach might be called a *functional programming style*.

Exercise 16-4

Write a "pure" version, `increment`, that creates and returns a new `MyTime` object rather than modifying the parameter.

Prototyping Versus Planning

Recall that the development plan I am demonstrating here is called "prototype and patch." For each function, I wrote a prototype that performed the basic calculation and then tested it, patching errors along the way.

This approach can be effective, especially if you don't yet have a deep understanding of the problem. But incremental corrections can generate code that is unnecessarily complicated, since it deals with many special cases, and unreliable, since it is hard to know if you have found all the errors.

An alternative is *designed development*, in which high-level insight into the problem can make the programming much easier. In this case, the insight is that a `Time` object is really a 3-digit number in base 60 (*http://bit.ly/2HYQLyI*). The `second` attribute is the "ones column," the `minute` attribute is the "sixties column," and the `hour` attribute is the "thirty-six hundreds column."

When we wrote addtime and increment!, we were effectively doing addition in base 60, which is why we had to carry from one column to the next.

This observation suggests another approach to the whole problem—we can convert MyTime objects to integers and take advantage of the fact that the computer knows how to do integer arithmetic.

Here is a function that converts MyTimes to integers:

```
function timetoint(time)
    minutes = time.hour * 60 + time.minute
    seconds = minutes * 60 + time.second
end
```

And here is a function that converts an integer to a MyTime (recall that divrem divides the first argument by the second and returns the quotient and remainder as a tuple):

```
function inttotime(seconds)
    (minutes, second) = divrem(seconds, 60)
    hour, minute = divrem(minutes, 60)
    MyTime(hour, minute, second)
end
```

You might have to think a bit, and run some tests, to convince yourself that these functions are correct. One way to test them is to check, for many values of x, that timetoint(inttotime(x)) == x. This is an example of a consistency check (see "Debugging" on page 137).

Once you are convinced they are correct, you can use them to rewrite addtime:

```
function addtime(t1, t2)
    seconds = timetoint(t1) + timetoint(t2)
    inttotime(seconds)
end
```

This version is shorter than the original, and easier to verify.

Exercise 16-5

Rewrite increment! using timetoint and inttotime.

In some ways, converting from base 60 to base 10 and back is harder than just dealing with times. Base conversion is more abstract; our intuition for dealing with time values is better.

But if we have the insight to treat times as base 60 numbers and make the investment of writing the conversion functions (timetoint and inttotime), we get a program that is shorter, easier to read and debug, and more reliable.

It is also easier to add features later. For example, imagine subtracting two MyTimes to find the duration between them. The naive approach would be to implement subtraction with borrowing. Using the conversion functions would be easier and more likely to be correct.

Ironically, sometimes making a problem harder (or more general) makes it easier (because there are fewer special cases and fewer opportunities for error).

Debugging

A `MyTime` object is well-formed if the values of `minute` and `second` are between 0 and 60 (including 0 but not 60) and if `hour` is positive. `hour` and `minute` should be integral values, but we might allow `second` to have a fraction part.

Requirements like these are called *invariants* because they should always be true. To put it a different way, if they are not true, something has gone wrong.

Writing code to check invariants can help detect errors and find their causes. For example, you might have a function like `isvalidtime` that takes a `MyTime` object and returns `false` if it violates an invariant:

```
function isvalidtime(time)
    if time.hour < 0 || time.minute < 0 || time.second < 0
        return false
    end
    if time.minute >= 60 || time.second >= 60
        return false
    end
    true
end
```

At the beginning of each function you could check the arguments to make sure they are valid:

```
function addtime(t1, t2)
    if !isvalidtime(t1) || !isvalidtime(t2)
        error("invalid MyTime object in add_time")
    end
    seconds = timetoint(t1) + timetoint(t2)
    inttotime(seconds)
end
```

Or you could use an `@assert` macro, which checks a given invariant and throws an exception if it fails:

```
function addtime(t1, t2)
    @assert(isvalidtime(t1) && isvalidtime(t2), "invalid MyTime object in
add_time")
    seconds = timetoint(t1) + timetoint(t2)
    inttotime(seconds)
end
```

`@assert` macros are useful because they distinguish code that deals with normal conditions from code that checks for errors.

Glossary

prototype and patch
> A development plan that involves writing a rough draft of a program, testing, and correcting errors as they are found.

pure function
> A function that does not modify any of the objects it receives as arguments. Most pure functions are fruitful.

modifier
> A function that changes one or more of the objects it receives as arguments. Most modifiers are void; that is, they return `nothing`.

functional programming style
> A style of program design in which the majority of functions are pure.

designed development
> A development plan that involves high-level insight into the problem and more planning than incremental development or prototype development.

invariant
> A condition that should never change during the execution of a program.

Exercises

Exercise 16-6

Write a function called `multime` that takes a `MyTime` object and a number and returns a new `MyTime` object that contains the product of the original `MyTime` and the number.

Then use `multime` to write a function that takes a `MyTime` object that represents the finishing time in a race and a number that represents the distance, and returns a `MyTime` object that represents the average pace (time per mile).

Exercise 16-7

Julia provides `Time` objects (*http://bit.ly/2CW6BWo*) that are similar to the `MyTime` objects in this chapter, but they provide a rich set of functions and operators.

1. Write a program that gets the current date and prints the day of the week.

2. Write a program that takes a birthday as input and prints the user's age and the number of days, hours, minutes, and seconds until her next birthday.

3. For two people born on different days, there is a day when one is twice as old as the other. That's their Double Day. Write a program that takes two birthdays and computes their Double Day.

4. For a little more challenge, write the more general version that computes the day when one person is n times older than the other.

CHAPTER 17

Multiple Dispatch

In Julia you have the ability to write code that can operate on different types. This is called "generic programming."

In this chapter I will discuss the use of type declarations in Julia, and I will introduce methods that offer ways to implement different behavior for a function depending on the types of their arguments. This is called "multiple dispatch."

Type Declarations

The `::` operator attaches *type annotations* to expressions and variables, indicating what types they should have:

```
julia> (1 + 2) :: Float64
ERROR: TypeError: in typeassert, expected Float64, got Int64
julia> (1 + 2) :: Int64
3
```

This helps to confirm that your program works the way you expect.

The `::` operator can also be appended to the lefthand side of an assignment, or included as part of a declaration:

```
julia> function returnfloat()
           x::Float64 = 100
           x
       end
returnfloat (generic function with 1 method)
julia> x = returnfloat()
100.0
julia> typeof(x)
Float64
```

The variable x is always of type Float64 and the value is converted to a floating point if needed.

A type annotation can also be attached to the header of a function definition:

```
function sinc(x)::Float64
    if x == 0
        return 1
    end
    sin(x)/(x)
end
```

The return value of sinc is always converted to type Float64.

The default behavior in Julia when types are omitted is to allow values to be of any type (Any).

Methods

In "Time" on page 189, we defined a struct named MyTime and you wrote a function named printtime:

```
using Printf

struct MyTime
    hour :: Int64
    minute :: Int64
    second :: Int64
end

function printtime(time)
    @printf("%02d:%02d:%02d", time.hour, time.minute, time.second)
end
```

As you can see, type declarations can (and should, for performance reasons) be added to the fields in a struct definition.

To call this function, we have to pass a MyTime object as an argument:

```
julia> start = MyTime(9, 45, 0)
MyTime(9, 45, 0)
julia> printtime(start)
09:45:00
```

To add a *method* to the function printtime that only accepts a MyTime object as an argument, all we have to do is append :: followed by MyTime to the argument time in the function definition:

```
function printtime(time::MyTime)
    @printf("%02d:%02d:%02d", time.hour, time.minute, time.second)
end
```

A method is a function definition with a specific *signature*: printtime has one argument of type MyTime.

Calling the function printtime with a MyTime object yields the same result as before:

```
julia> printtime(start)
09:45:00
```

We can now redefine the first method without the :: type annotation, allowing an argument of any type:

```
function printtime(time)
    println("I don't know how to print the argument time.")
end
```

If you call the function printtime with an object that isn't a MyTime object, you now get:

```
julia> printtime(150)
I don't know how to print the argument time.
```

Exercise 17-1

Rewrite timetoint and inttotime (from "Prototyping Versus Planning" on page 192) to specify their arguments.

Additional Examples

Here's a version of increment (from "Modifiers" on page 191) rewritten to specify its arguments:

```
function increment(time::MyTime, seconds::Int64)
    seconds += timetoint(time)
    inttotime(seconds)
end
```

Note that now it is a pure function, not a modifier.

Here's how you would invoke increment:

```
julia> start = MyTime(9, 45, 0)
MyTime(9, 45, 0)
julia> increment(start, 1337)
MyTime(10, 7, 17)
```

If you put the arguments in the wrong order, you get an error:

```
julia> increment(1337, start)
ERROR: MethodError: no method matching increment(::Int64, ::MyTime)
```

The signature of the method is increment(time::MyTime, seconds::Int64), not increment(seconds::Int64, time::MyTime).

Rewriting `isafter` to act only on `MyTime` objects is as easy:

```
function isafter(t1::MyTime, t2::MyTime)
    (t1.hour, t1.minute, t1.second) > (t2.hour, t2.minute, t2.second)
end
```

By the way, optional arguments are implemented as syntax for multiple method definitions. For example, this definition:

```
function f(a=1, b=2)
    a + 2b
end
```

translates to the following three methods:

```
f(a, b) = a + 2b
f(a) = f(a, 2)
f() = f(1, 2)
```

These expressions are valid Julia method definitions. This is shorthand notation for defining functions/methods.

Constructors

A *constructor* is a special function that is called to create an object. The *default constructor* methods of `MyTime`, which take all fields as parameters, have the following signatures:

```
MyTime(hour, minute, second)
MyTime(hour::Int64, minute::Int64, second::Int64)
```

We can also add our own *outer constructor* methods:

```
function MyTime(time::MyTime)
    MyTime(time.hour, time.minute, time.second)
end
```

This method is called a *copy constructor* because the new `MyTime` object is a copy of its argument.

To enforce invariants, we need *inner constructor* methods:

```
struct MyTime
    hour :: Int64
    minute :: Int64
    second :: Int64
    function MyTime(hour::Int64=0, minute::Int64=0, second::Int64=0)
        @assert(0 ≤ minute < 60, "Minute is not between 0 and 60.")
        @assert(0 ≤ second < 60, "Second is not between 0 and 60.")
        new(hour, minute, second)
    end
end
```

The struct MyTime now has four inner constructor methods:

```
MyTime()
MyTime(hour::Int64)
MyTime(hour::Int64, minute::Int64)
MyTime(hour::Int64, minute::Int64, second::Int64)
```

An inner constructor method is always defined inside the block of a type declaration, and it has access to a special function called new that creates objects of the newly declared type.

The default constructor is not available if any inner constructor is defined. You have to write explicitly all the inner constructors you need.

A second method without arguments of the local function new exists:

```
struct MyTime
    hour :: Int
    minute :: Int
    second :: Int
    function MyTime(hour::Int64=0, minute::Int64=0, second::Int64=0)
        @assert(0 ≤ minute < 60, "Minute is between 0 and 60.")
        @assert(0 ≤ second < 60, "Second is between 0 and 60.")
        time = new()
        time.hour = hour
        time.minute = minute
        time.second = second
        time
    end
end
```

This allows us to construct recursive data structures—i.e., structs where one of the fields is the struct itself. In this case the struct has to be mutable because its fields are modified after instantiation.

show

show is a special function that returns a string representation of an object. For example, here is a show method for MyTime objects:

```
using Printf

function Base.show(io::IO, time::MyTime)
    @printf(io, "%02d:%02d:%02d", time.hour, time.minute, time.second)
end
```

The prefix `Base` is needed because we want to add a new method to the `Base.show` function.

When you print an object, Julia invokes the `show` function:

```julia
julia> time = MyTime(9, 45)
09:45:00
```

When I write a new composite type, I almost always start by writing an outer constructor, which makes it easier to instantiate objects, and a `show` method, which is useful for debugging.

Exercise 17-2

Write an outer constructor method for the `Point` class that takes x and y as optional parameters and assigns them to the corresponding fields.

Operator Overloading

By defining operator methods, you can specify the behavior of operators on programmer-defined types. For example, if you define a method named + with two `MyTime` arguments, you can use the + operator on `MyTime` objects.

Here is what the definition might look like:

```julia
import Base.+

function +(t1::MyTime, t2::MyTime)
    seconds = timetoint(t1) + timetoint(t2)
    inttotime(seconds)
end
```

The `import` statement adds the + operator to the local scope so that methods can be added.

And here is how you could use it:

```julia
julia> start = MyTime(9, 45)
09:45:00
julia> duration = MyTime(1, 35, 0)
01:35:00
julia> start + duration
11:20:00
```

When you apply the + operator to `MyTime` objects, Julia invokes the newly added method. When the REPL shows the result, Julia invokes `show`. So, there is a lot happening behind the scenes!

Adding to the behavior of an operator so that it works with programmer-defined types is called *operator overloading*.

Multiple Dispatch

In the previous section we added two `MyTime` objects, but you also might want to add an integer to a `MyTime` object:

```
function +(time::MyTime, seconds::Int64)
    increment(time, seconds)
end
```

Here is an example that uses the + operator with a `MyTime` object and an integer:

```
julia> start = MyTime(9, 45)
09:45:00
julia> start + 1337
10:07:17
```

Addition is a commutative operator, so we have to add another method:

```
function +(seconds::Int64, time::MyTime)
    time + seconds
end
```

And we get the same result:

```
julia> 1337 + start
10:07:17
```

The *dispatch* mechanism determines which method to execute when a function is called. Julia allows the dispatch process to choose which of a function's methods to call based on the number of arguments given, and on the types of all of the function's arguments. Using all of a function's arguments to choose which method should be invoked is known as *multiple dispatch*.

Exercise 17-3

Write + methods for `Point` objects:

- If both operands are `Point` objects, the method should return a new `Point` object whose x coordinate is the sum of the x coordinates of the operands, and likewise for the y coordinates.
- If the first or the second operand is a tuple, the method should add the first element of the tuple to the x coordinate and the second element to the y coordinate, and return a new `Point` object with the result.

Generic Programming

Multiple dispatch is useful when it is necessary, but (fortunately) it is not always necessary. Often you can avoid it by writing functions that work correctly for arguments with different types. This is known as *generic programming*.

Many of the functions we wrote for strings also work for other sequence types. For example, in "Dictionaries as Collections of Counters" on page 129 we used histogram to count the number of times each letter appears in a word:

```
function histogram(s)
    d = Dict()
    for c in s
        if c ∉ keys(d)
            d[c] = 1
        else
            d[c] += 1
        end
    end
    d
end
```

This function also works for lists, tuples, and even dictionaries, as long as the elements of s are hashable so they can be used as keys in d:

```
julia> t = ("spam", "egg", "spam", "spam", "bacon", "spam")
("spam", "egg", "spam", "spam", "bacon", "spam")
julia> histogram(t)
Dict{Any,Any} with 3 entries:
  "bacon" => 1
  "spam"  => 4
  "egg"   => 1
```

Functions that work with several types are called *polymorphic*. Polymorphism can facilitate code reuse.

For example, the built-in function sum, which adds the elements of a sequence, works as long as the elements of the sequence support addition.

Since a + method is provided for MyTime objects, they work with sum:

```
julia> t1 = MyTime(1, 7, 2)
01:07:02
julia> t2 = MyTime(1, 5, 8)
01:05:08
julia> t3 = MyTime(1, 5, 0)
01:05:00
julia> sum((t1, t2, t3))
03:17:10
```

In general, if all of the operations inside a function work with a given type, the function works with that type.

The best kind of polymorphism is the unintentional kind, where you discover that a function you already wrote can be applied to a type you never planned for.

Interface and Implementation

One of the goals of multiple dispatch is to make software more maintainable, which means that you can keep the program working when other parts of the system change, and modify the program to meet new requirements.

A design principle that helps achieve that goal is to keep interfaces separate from implementations. This means that the methods having an argument annotated with a type should not depend on how the fields of that type are represented.

For example, in this chapter we developed a struct that represents a time of day. Methods having an argument annotated with this type include timetoint, isafter, and +.

We could implement those methods in several ways. The details of the implementation depend on how we represent MyTime. In this chapter, the fields of a MyTime object are hour, minute, and second.

As an alternative, we could replace these fields with a single integer representing the number of seconds since midnight. This implementation would make some functions, like isafter, easier to write, but other functions harder.

After you deploy a new type, you might discover a better implementation. If other parts of the program are using your type, it might be time-consuming and error-prone to change the interface.

But if you designed the interface carefully, you can change the implementation without changing the interface, which means that other parts of the program don't have to change.

Debugging

Calling a function with the correct arguments can be difficult when more than one method for the function is specified. To help with this, Julia allows us to introspect the signatures of the methods of a function.

To know what methods are available for a given function, you can use the function methods:

```
julia> methods(printtime)
# 2 methods for generic function "printtime":
[1] printtime(time::MyTime) in Main at REPL[3]:2
[2] printtime(time) in Main at REPL[4]:2
```

In this example, the function `printtime` has two methods: one with a `MyTime` argument and one with an `Any` argument.

Glossary

type annotation
:   The operator :: followed by a type, indicating that an expression or a variable is of that type.

method
:   A definition of a possible behavior for a function.

signature
:   The number and type of the arguments of a method, allowing the dispatch to select the most specific method of a function during the function call.

constructor
:   A special function called to create an object.

default constructor
:   An inner constructor that is available when no programmer-defined inner constructors are provided.

outer constructor
:   A constructor defined outside the type definition to define convenience methods for creating an object.

copy constructor
:   An outer constructor method of a type with as its only argument an object of the type. It creates a new object that is a copy of the argument.

inner constructor
:   A constructor defined inside the type definition to enforce invariants or to construct self-referential objects.

operator overloading
:   Adding to the behavior of an operator like + so it works with a programmer-defined type.

dispatch
:   The choice of which method to execute when a function is executed.

multiple dispatch
:   Dispatch based on all of a function's arguments.

generic programming
:   Writing code that can work with more than one type.

polymorphic function
    A function whose argument(s) can be of several types.

Exercises

Exercise 17-4

Change the fields of MyTime to be a single integer representing seconds since midnight. Then modify the methods defined in this chapter to work with the new implementation.

Exercise 17-5

Write a definition for a type named Kangaroo with a field named pouchcontents of type Array and the following methods:

- A constructor that initializes pouchcontents to an empty array

- A method named putinpouch that takes a Kangaroo object and an object of any type and adds it to pouchcontents

- A show method that returns a string representation of the Kangaroo object and the contents of the pouch

Test your code by creating two Kangaroo objects, assigning them to variables named kanga and roo, and then adding roo to the contents of kanga's pouch.

CHAPTER 18

Subtyping

In the previous chapter we introduced the multiple dispatch mechanism and polymorphic methods. Not specifying the types of the arguments results in a method that can be called with arguments of any type. Specifying a subset of allowed types in the signature of a method is a logical next step.

In this chapter I demonstrate subtyping using types that represent playing cards, decks of cards, and poker hands.

If you don't play poker, you can read about it (*http://bit.ly/2VmIfMT*), but you don't have to; I'll tell you what you need to know for the exercises.

Cards

There are 52 cards in a deck, each of which belongs to one of 4 suits and one of 13 ranks. The suits are Spades (♠), Hearts (♥), Diamonds (♦), and Clubs (♣). The ranks are Ace (A), 2, 3, 4, 5, 6, 7, 8, 9, 10, Jack (J), Queen (Q), and King (K). Depending on the game that you are playing, an Ace may be higher than a King or lower than a 2.

If we want to define a new object to represent a playing card, it is obvious what the attributes should be: rank and suit. It is not as obvious what type the attributes should be. One possibility is to use strings containing words like "Spade" for suits and "Queen" for ranks. One problem with this implementation is that it would not be easy to compare cards to see which had a higher rank or suit.

An alternative is to use integers to *encode* the ranks and suits. In this context, "encode" means that we are going to define a mapping between numbers and suits, or between numbers and ranks. This kind of encoding is not meant to be a secret (that would be "encryption").

For example, we might map the suits to integer codes as follows:

- ♠ ⟼ 4
- ♥ ⟼ 3
- ♦ ⟼ 2
- ♣ ⟼ 1

This makes it easy to compare cards; because higher suits map to higher numbers, we can compare suits by comparing their codes.

I am using the ⟼ symbol to make it clear that these mappings are not part of the Julia program. They are part of the program design, but they don't appear explicitly in the code.

The struct definition for Card looks like this:

```
struct Card
    suit :: Int64
    rank :: Int64
    function Card(suit::Int64, rank::Int64)
        @assert(1 ≤ suit ≤ 4, "suit is not between 1 and 4")
        @assert(1 ≤ rank ≤ 13, "rank is not between 1 and 13")
        new(suit, rank)
    end
end
```

To create a Card, you call Card with the suit and rank of the card you want:

```
julia> queen_of_diamonds = Card(2, 12)
Card(2, 12)
```

Global Variables

In order to print Card objects in a way that people can easily read, we need a mapping from the integer codes to the corresponding ranks and suits. A natural way to do that is with arrays of strings:

```
const suit_names = ["♣", "♦", "♥", "♠"]
const rank_names = ["A", "2", "3", "4", "5", "6", "7", "8", "9", "10", "J",
                    "Q", "K"]
```

The variables suit_names and rank_names are global variables. The const declaration means that the variable can only be assigned once. This solves the performance problem of global variables.

Now we can implement an appropriate show method:

```
function Base.show(io::IO, card::Card)
    print(io, rank_names[card.rank], suit_names[card.suit])
end
```

The expression rank_names[card.rank] means "use the field rank from the object card as an index into the array rank_names, and select the appropriate string."

With the methods we have so far, we can create and print Card:

```julia
julia> Card(3, 11)
J♥
```

Comparing Cards

For built-in types, there are relational operators (<, >, ==, etc.) that compare values and determine when one is greater than, less than, or equal to another. For programmer-defined types, we can override the behavior of the built-in operators by providing a method named <.

The correct ordering for cards is not obvious. For example, which is better, the 3 of Clubs or the 2 of Diamonds? One has a higher rank, but the other has a higher suit. In order to compare cards, you have to decide whether rank or suit is more important.

The answer might depend on what game you are playing, but to keep things simple, we'll make the arbitrary choice that suit is more important, so all of the Spades outrank all of the Diamonds and so on.

With that decided, we can write <:

```julia
import Base.isless

function isless(c1::Card, c2::Card)
    (c1.suit, c1.rank) < (c2.suit, c2.rank)
end
```

Exercise 18-1

Write a < method for MyTime objects. You can use tuple comparison, but you also might consider comparing integers.

Unit Testing

Unit testing allows you to verify the correctness of your code by comparing the results of your code to what you expect. This can be useful to be sure that your code is still correct after modifications, and it is also a way to predefine the correct behavior of your code during development.

Simple unit testing can be performed with the @test macro:

```julia
julia> using Test

julia> @test Card(1, 4) < Card(2, 4)
```

```
Test Passed
julia> @test Card(1, 3) < Card(1, 4)
Test Passed
```

@test returns a "Test Passed" if the expression following it is true, a "Test Failed" if it is false, and an "Error Result" if it could not be evaluated.

Decks

Now that we have Cards, the next step is to define Decks. Since a deck is made up of cards, it is natural for each Deck to contain an array of Cards as an attribute.

The following is a struct definition for Deck. The constructor creates the field cards and generates the standard set of 52 Cards:

```
struct Deck
    cards :: Array{Card, 1}
end

function Deck()
    deck = Deck(Card[])
    for suit in 1:4
        for rank in 1:13
            push!(deck.cards, Card(suit, rank))
        end
    end
    deck
end
```

The easiest way to populate the deck is with a nested loop. The outer loop enumerates the suits from 1 to 4. The inner loop enumerates the ranks from 1 to 13. Each iteration creates a new Card with the current suit and rank, and pushes it to deck.cards.

Here is a show method for Deck:

```
function Base.show(io::IO, deck::Deck)
    for card in deck.cards
        print(io, card, " ")
    end
    println()
end
```

Here's what the result looks like:

```
julia> Deck()
A♣ 2♣ 3♣ 4♣ 5♣ 6♣ 7♣ 8♣ 9♣ 10♣ J♣ Q♣ K♣ A♦ 2♦ 3♦ 4♦ 5♦ 6♦ 7♦ 8♦ 9♦ 10♦ J♦ Q♦
K♦ A♥ 2♥ 3♥ 4♥ 5♥ 6♥ 7♥ 8♥ 9♥ 10♥ J♥ Q♥ K♥ A♠ 2♠ 3♠ 4♠ 5♠ 6♠ 7♠ 8♠ 9♠ 10♠ J♠ Q♠
K♠
```

Add, Remove, Shuffle, and Sort

To deal cards, we would like a function that removes a Card from the Deck and returns it. The function pop! provides a convenient way to do that:

```
function Base.pop!(deck::Deck)
    pop!(deck.cards)
end
```

Since pop! removes the last Card in the array, we are dealing from the bottom of the Deck.

To add a Card, we can use the function push!:

```
function Base.push!(deck::Deck, card::Card)
    push!(deck.cards, card)
    deck
end
```

A method like this that uses another method without doing much work is sometimes called a *veneer*. The metaphor comes from woodworking, where a veneer is a thin layer of good-quality wood glued to the surface of a cheaper piece of wood to improve the appearance.

In this case push! is a "thin" method that expresses an array operation in terms appropriate for decks. It improves the appearance, or interface, of the implementation.

As another example, we can write a method named shuffle! using the function Random.shuffle!:

```
using Random

function Random.shuffle!(deck::Deck)
    shuffle!(deck.cards)
    deck
end
```

Exercise 18-2

Write a function named sort! that uses the function sort! to sort the cards in a Deck. sort! uses the < method we defined to determine the order.

Abstract Types and Subtyping

We want a type to represent a "hand"; that is, the cards held by one player. A hand is similar to a deck: both are made up of a collection of cards, and both require operations like adding and removing cards.

A hand is also different from a deck; there are operations we want for hands that don't make sense for a deck. For example, in poker we might compare two hands to see which one wins. In bridge, we might compute a score for a hand in order to make a bid.

So, we need a way to group related *concrete types*. In Julia this is done by defining an *abstract type* that serves as a parent for both Deck and Hand. This is called *subtyping*.

Let's call this abstract type CardSet:

```
abstract type CardSet end
```

A new abstract type is created with the `abstract type` keyword. An optional "parent" type can be specified by putting <: after the name, followed by the name of an already existing abstract type.

When no *supertype* is given, the default supertype is Any—a predefined abstract type that all objects are instances of and all types are subtypes of.

We can now express that Deck is a descendant of CardSet:

```
struct Deck <: CardSet
    cards :: Array{Card, 1}
end

function Deck()
    deck = Deck(Card[])
    for suit in 1:4
        for rank in 1:13
            push!(deck.cards, Card(suit, rank))
        end
    end
    deck
end
```

The operator `isa` checks whether an object is of a given type:

```
julia> deck = Deck();

julia> deck isa CardSet
true
```

A hand is also a kind of CardSet:

```
struct Hand <: CardSet
    cards :: Array{Card, 1}
    label :: String
end

function Hand(label::String="")
    Hand(Card[], label)
end
```

Instead of populating the hand with 52 new `Cards`, the constructor for `Hand` initializes `cards` with an empty array. An optional argument can be passed to the constructor giving a label to the `Hand`:

```
julia> hand = Hand("new hand")
Hand(Card[], "new hand")
```

Abstract Types and Functions

We can now express the common operations between `Deck` and `Hand` as functions having a `CardSet` as an argument:

```
function Base.show(io::IO, cs::CardSet)
    for card in cs.cards
        print(io, card, " ")
    end
end

function Base.pop!(cs::CardSet)
    pop!(cs.cards)
end

function Base.push!(cs::CardSet, card::Card)
    push!(cs.cards, card)
    nothing
end
```

We can use pop! and push! to deal a card:

```
julia> deck = Deck()
A♣ 2♣ 3♣ 4♣ 5♣ 6♣ 7♣ 8♣ 9♣ 10♣ J♣ Q♣ K♣ A♦ 2♦ 3♦ 4♦ 5♦ 6♦ 7♦ 8♦ 9♦ 10♦ J♦ Q♦
K♦ A♥ 2♥ 3♥ 4♥ 5♥ 6♥ 7♥ 8♥ 9♥ 10♥ J♥ Q♥ K♥ A♠ 2♠ 3♠ 4♠ 5♠ 6♠ 7♠ 8♠ 9♠ 10♠ J♠ Q♠
K♠
julia> shuffle!(deck)
4♠ Q♦ A♣ 9♦ Q♣ 6♣ 10♣ Q♥ A♦ 8♥ 9♥ Q♠ 4♦ 5♥ 9♠ 10♥ A♠ 7♣ 2♠ 5♠ 2♦ K♠ J♠ 10♠ 7♦
2♥ 3♦ 7♠ 8♦ A♥ K♥ 7♥ J♥ 6♦ J♦ 6♥ K♦ 8♠ 5♦ 4♥ 8♣ J♣ 9♣ 3♠ 2♣ K♣ 3♥ 5♣ 6♠ 10♦ 4♣
3♣
julia> card = pop!(deck)
3♣
julia> push!(hand, card)
```

A natural next step is to encapsulate this code in a function called move!:

```
function move!(cs1::CardSet, cs2::CardSet, n::Int)
    @assert 1 ≤ n ≤ length(cs1.cards)
    for i in 1:n
        card = pop!(cs1)
        push!(cs2, card)
    end
    nothing
end
```

move! takes three arguments, two CardSet objects and the number of cards to deal. It modifies both CardSet objects, and returns nothing.

In some games, cards are moved from one hand to another, or from a hand back to the deck. You can use move! for any of these operations: cs1 and cs2 can be either a Deck or a Hand.

Type Diagrams

So far we have seen stack diagrams, which show the state of a program, and object diagrams, which show the attributes of an object and their values. These diagrams represent a snapshot of the execution of a program, so they change as the program runs.

They are also highly detailed—for some purposes, too detailed. A *type diagram* is a more abstract representation of the structure of a program. Instead of showing individual objects, it shows types and the relationships between them.

There are several kinds of relationships between types:

- Objects of a concrete type might contain references to objects of another type. For example, each Rectangle contains a reference to a Point, and each Deck contains references to an array of Cards. This kind of relationship is called *has-a*, as in, "a Rectangle has a Point."

- A concrete type can have an abstract type as a supertype. This relationship is called *is-a*, as in, "a Hand is a kind of a CardSet."

- One type might depend on another, in the sense that objects of one type take objects of the second type as parameters, or use objects of the second type as part of a computation. This kind of relationship is called a *dependency*.

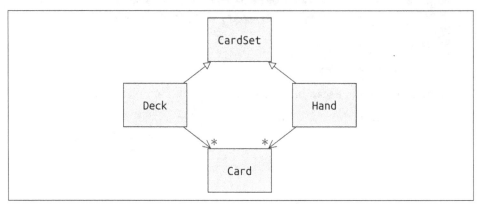

Figure 18-1. Type diagram

The arrow with a hollow triangle head represents an is-a relationship; in this case it indicates that Hand has CardSet as a supertype.

The standard arrowhead represents a has-a relationship; in this case a Deck has references to Card objects.

The star (*) near the arrowhead is a *multiplicity*; it indicates how many Cards a Deck has. A multiplicity can be a simple number, like 52; a range, like 5:7; or a star, which indicates that a Deck can have any number of Cards.

There are no dependencies in this diagram. They would normally be shown with a dashed arrow. Or if there are a lot of dependencies, they are sometimes omitted.

A more detailed diagram might show that a Deck actually contains an array of Cards, but built-in types like array and dictionaries are usually not included in type diagrams.

Debugging

Subtyping can make debugging difficult because when you call a function with an object as an argument, it might be hard to figure out which method will be invoked.

Suppose you are writing a function that works with Hand objects. You would like it to work with all kinds of Hands, like PokerHands, BridgeHands, etc. If you invoke a method like sort!, you might get the version defined for an abstract type Hand, but if a method sort! with any of the subtypes as an argument exists, you'll get that version instead. This behavior is usually a good thing, but it can be confusing:

```
function Base.sort!(hand::Hand)
    sort!(hand.cards)
end
```

Any time you are unsure about the flow of execution through your program, the simplest solution is to add print statements at the beginning of the relevant methods. If shuffle! prints a message that says something like Running shuffle! Deck, then as the program runs it traces the flow of execution.

As a better alternative, you can use the @which macro:

```
julia> @which sort!(hand)
sort!(hand::Hand) in Main at REPL[5]:1
```

This tells us that the sort! method for hand is the one having as an argument an object of type Hand.

Here's a design suggestion: when you override a method, the interface of the new method should be the same as the old one. It should take the same parameters, return the same type, and obey the same preconditions and postconditions. If you follow this rule, you will find that any function designed to work with an instance of a super-type, like a `CardSet`, will also work with instances of its subtypes (`Deck` and `Hand`).

If you violate this rule, which is called the "Liskov substitution principle," your code will collapse like (sorry) a house of cards.

The function `supertype` can be used to find the direct supertype of a type:

```
julia> supertype(Deck)
CardSet
```

Data Encapsulation

The previous chapters demonstrated a development plan we might call "type-oriented design." We identified objects we needed—like `Point`, `Rectangle`, and `MyTime`—and defined structs to represent them. In each case there was an obvious correspondence between the object and some entity in the real world (or at least a mathematical world).

But sometimes it is less obvious what objects you need and how they should interact. In that case you need a different development plan. In the same way that we discovered function interfaces by encapsulation and generalization, we can discover type interfaces by *data encapsulation*.

Markov analysis, described in "Markov Analysis" on page 159, provides a good example. If you look at my solution (*http://bit.ly/2OM9myx*) to "Exercise 13-8" on page 160, you'll see that it uses two global variables—`suffixes` and `prefix`—that are read and written from several functions:

```
suffixes = Dict()
prefix = []
```

Because these variables are global, we can only run one analysis at a time. If we read two texts, their prefixes and suffixes would be added to the same data structures (which makes for some interesting generated text).

To run multiple analyses, and keep them separate, we can encapsulate the state of each analysis in an object. Here's what that looks like:

```
struct Markov
    order :: Int64
    suffixes :: Dict{Tuple{String,Vararg{String}}, Array{String, 1}}
    prefix :: Array{String, 1}
end

function Markov(order::Int64=2)
    new(order, Dict{Tuple{String,Vararg{String}}, Array{String, 1}}(),
Array{String, 1}())
end
```

Next, we transform the functions into methods. For example, here's processword:

```
function processword(markov::Markov, word::String)
    if length(markov.prefix) < markov.order
        push!(markov.prefix, word)
        return
    end
    get!(markov.suffixes, (markov.prefix...,), Array{String, 1}())
    push!(markov.suffixes[(markov.prefix...,)], word)
    popfirst!(markov.prefix)
    push!(markov.prefix, word)
end
```

Transforming a program like this—changing the design without changing the behavior—is another example of refactoring (see "Refactoring" on page 41).

This example suggests a development plan for designing types:

- Start by writing functions that read and write global variables (when necessary).
- Once you get the program working, look for associations between global variables and the functions that use them.
- Encapsulate related variables as fields of a struct.
- Transform the associated functions into methods with as argument objects of the new type.

Exercise 18-3

Download my Markov code from GitHub (*http://bit.ly/2OM9myx*), and follow the steps described here to encapsulate the global variables as attributes of a new struct called Markov.

Glossary

encode
> To represent one set of values using another set of values by constructing a mapping between them.

unit testing
> A standardized way to test the correctness of code.

veneer
> A method or function that provides a different interface to another function without doing much computation.

concrete type
> A type that can be constructed.

abstract type
>A type that can act as a parent for another type.

subtyping
>The ability to define a hierarchy of related types.

supertype
>An abstract type that is the parent of another type.

subtype
>A type that has as its parent an abstract type.

type diagram
>A diagram that shows the types in a program and the relationships between them.

has-a relationship
>A relationship between two types where instances of one type contain references to instances of the other.

is-a relationship
>A relationship between a subtype and its supertype.

dependency
>A relationship between two types where instances of one type use instances of the other type, but do not store them as fields.

multiplicity
>A notation in a type diagram that shows, for a has-a relationship, how many references there are to instances of another class.

data encapsulation
>A program development plan that involves a prototype using global variables and a final version that makes the global variables into instance fields.

Exercises

Exercise 18-4

For the following program, draw a type diagram that shows these types and the relationships among them.

```
abstract type PingPongParent end

struct Ping <: PingPongParent
    pong :: PingPongParent
end
```

```
struct Pong <: PingPongParent
    pings :: Array{Ping, 1}
    function Pong(pings=Array{Ping, 1}())
        new(pings)
    end
end

function addping(pong::Pong, ping::Ping)
    push!(pong.pings, ping)
    nothing
end

pong = Pong()
ping = Ping(pong)
addping(pong, ping)
```

Exercise 18-5

Write a method called deal! that takes three parameters: a Deck, the number of
Hands, and the number of Cards per Hand. It should create the appropriate number of
Hand objects, deal the appropriate number of Cards per Hand, and return an array of
Hands.

Exercise 18-6

The following are the possible hands in poker, in increasing order of value and
decreasing order of probability:

Pair
> Two cards with the same rank

Two pair
> Two pairs of cards with the same rank

Three of a kind
> Three cards with the same rank

Straight
> Five cards with ranks in sequence (Aces can be high or low, so Ace-2-3-4-5 is a
> straight and so is 10-Jack-Queen-King-Ace, but Queen-King-Ace-2-3 is not)

Flush
> Five cards with the same suit

Full house
> Three cards with one rank, two cards with another

Four of a kind
> Four cards with the same rank

Straight flush

Five cards in sequence (as defined previously) and with the same suit

The goal of this exercise is to estimate the probability of drawing these various hands.

1. Add methods named `haspair`, `hastwopair`, etc., that return `true` or `false` according to whether or not the hand meets the relevant criteria. Your code should work correctly for hands that contain any number of cards (although five and seven are the most common sizes).

2. Write a method named `classify` that figures out the highest-value classification for a hand and sets the `label` field accordingly. For example, a seven-card hand might contain a flush and a pair; it should be labeled `flush`.

3. When you are convinced that your classification methods are working, the next step is to estimate the probabilities of the various hands. Write a function that shuffles a deck of cards, divides it into hands, classifies the hands, and counts the number of times various classifications appear.

4. Print a table of the classifications and their probabilities. Run your program with larger and larger numbers of hands until the output values converge to a reasonable degree of accuracy. Compare your results to these hand ranks (*http://bit.ly/ 2G37nDb*).

CHAPTER 19

The Goodies: Syntax

One of my goals for this book has been to teach you as little Julia as possible. When there were two ways to do something, I picked one and avoided mentioning the other. Or sometimes I put the second one into an exercise.

Now I want to go back for some of the good bits that got left behind. Julia provides a number of features that are not really necessary—you can write good code without them—but with them you can sometimes write code that's more concise, readable, or efficient (and sometimes all three).

This chapter and the next discuss the things I have left out in the previous chapters:

- Syntax supplements
- Functions, types, and macros directly available in `Base`
- Functions, types, and macros in the standard library

Named Tuples

You can name the components of a tuple, creating a *named tuple*:

```julia
julia> x = (a=1, b=1+1)
(a = 1, b = 2)
julia> x.a
1
```

With named tuples, fields can be accessed by name using dot syntax (`x.a`).

Functions

A function in Julia can be defined by a compact syntax:

```
julia> f(x,y) = x + y
f (generic function with 1 method)
```

Anonymous Functions

We can define a function without specifying a name:

```
julia> x -> x^2 + 2x - 1
#1 (generic function with 1 method)
julia> function (x)
            x^2 + 2x - 1
       end
#3 (generic function with 1 method)
```

These are examples of *anonymous functions*. Anonymous functions are often used as arguments to another function:

```
julia> using Plots

julia> plot(x -> x^2 + 2x - 1, 0, 10, xlabel="x", ylabel="y")
```

Figure 19-1 shows the output of the plotting command.

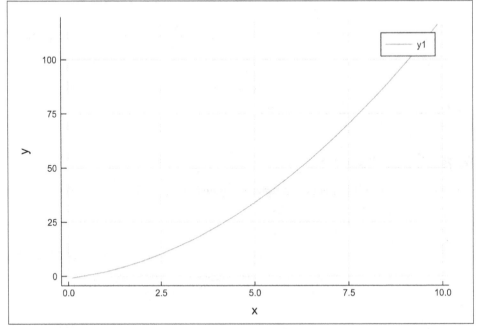

Figure 19-1. Plot

Keyword Arguments

Function arguments can also be named:

```
julia> function myplot(x, y; style="solid", width=1, color="black")
          ###
       end
myplot (generic function with 1 method)
julia> myplot(0:10, 0:10, style="dotted", color="blue")
```

Keyword arguments in a function are specified after a semicolon in the signature but can also be called with a comma.

Closures

A *closure* is a technique allowing a function to capture a variable defined outside the calling scope of the function:

```
julia> foo(x) = ()->x
foo (generic function with 1 method)
julia> bar = foo(1)
#1 (generic function with 1 method)
julia> bar()
1
```

In this example, the function `foo` returns an anonymous function that has access to the `x` argument of the function `foo`. `bar` points to the anonymous function and returns the value of the argument of `foo`.

Blocks

A *block* is a way to group a number of statements. A block starts with the keyword `begin` and ends with `end`.

In Chapter 4, the `@svg` macro was introduced:

```
🐢 Turtle()
@svg begin
    forward(🐢, 100)
    turn(🐢, -90)
    forward(🐢, 100)
end
```

In this example the macro `@svg` has a single argument, a block grouping three function calls.

let Blocks

A *let block* is useful to create new bindings—i.e., locations that can refer to values:

```
julia> x, y, z = -1, -1, -1;

julia> let x = 1, z
           @show x y z;
       end
x = 1
y = -1
ERROR: UndefVarError: z not defined
julia> @show x y z;
x = -1
y = -1
z = -1
```

In this example, the first @show macro shows the local variable x, the global variable y, and the undefined local variable z. As the second @show macro shows, the global variables are untouched.

do Blocks

In "Reading and Writing" on page 168 I showed you how to close a file when you're done writing. This can be done automatically using a *do block*:

```
julia> data = "This here's the wattle,\nthe emblem of our land.\n"
"This here's the wattle,\nthe emblem of our land.\n"
julia> open("output.txt", "w") do fout
           write(fout, data)
       end
48
```

In this example fout is the file stream used for output.

This is functionally equivalent to:

```
julia> f = fout -> begin
           write(fout, data)
       end
#3 (generic function with 1 method)
julia> open(f, "output.txt", "w")
48
```

The anonymous function is used as the first argument of the function open:

```
function open(f::Function, args...)
    io = open(args...)
    try
        f(io)
    finally
        close(io)
    end
end
```

A do block can "capture" variables from its enclosing scope. For example, the variable data in the open ... do example is captured from the outer scope.

Control Flow

In the previous chapters we used `if-elseif` statements to make choices. Ternary operators and short-circuit evaluations are more compact ways to do the same. A task is an advanced control structure that directly modifies the flow of the program.

Ternary Operator

The *ternary operator*, `?:`, is an alternative to an `if-elseif` statement used when you need to make a choice between single expression values:

```
julia> a = 150
150
julia> a % 2 == 0 ? println("even") : println("odd")
even
```

The expression before the `?` is a conditional expression. If the condition is `true`, the expression before the `:` is evaluated; otherwise, the expression after the `:` is evaluated.

Short-Circuit Evaluation

The operators `&&` and `||` do a *short-circuit evaluation*: the next argument is only evaluated when it is needed to determine the final value.

For example, a recursive factorial routine could be defined like this:

```
function fact(n::Integer)
    n >= 0 || error("n must be non-negative")
    n == 0 && return 1
    n * fact(n-1)
end
```

Tasks (aka Coroutines)

A *task* is a control structure that can pass control cooperatively without returning. In Julia, a task can be implemented as a function having as its first argument a `Channel` object. A `Channel` is used to pass values from the function to the callee.

The Fibonacci sequence can be generated using a task:

```
function fib(c::Channel)
    a = 0
    b = 1
    put!(c, a)
    while true
        put!(c, b)
        (a, b) = (b, a+b)
    end
end
```

put! stores values in a `Channel` object and `take!` reads values from it:

```
julia> fib_gen = Channel(fib);

julia> take!(fib_gen)
0
julia> take!(fib_gen)
1
julia> take!(fib_gen)
1
julia> take!(fib_gen)
2
julia> take!(fib_gen)
3
```

The constructor `Channel` creates the task. The function `fib` is suspended after each call to put! and resumed after `take!`. For performance reasons, several values of the sequence are buffered in the `Channel` object during a resume/suspend cycle.

A `Channel` object can also be used as an iterator:

```
julia> for val in Channel(fib)
           print(val, " ")
           val > 20 && break
       end
0 1 1 2 3 5 8 13 21
```

Types

Structs are the only user-defined types we have defined. Julia provides some extensions (primitive types, parametric types, and type unions), giving more flexibility to the programmer.

Primitive Types

A concrete type consisting of plain old bits is called a *primitive type*. Unlike most languages, Julia allows you to declare your own primitive types. The standard primitive types are defined in the same way:

```
primitive type Float64 <: AbstractFloat 64 end
primitive type Bool <: Integer 8 end
primitive type Char <: AbstractChar 32 end
primitive type Int64 <: Signed 64 end
```

The number in the statement specifies how many bits are required.

The following example creates a primitive type `Byte` and a constructor:

```
julia> primitive type Byte 8 end

julia> Byte(val::UInt8) = reinterpret(Byte, val)
```

```
Byte
julia> b = Byte(0x01)
Byte(0x01)
```

The function `reinterpret` is used to store the bits of an unsigned integer with 8 bits (`UInt8`) into the `Byte`.

Parametric Types

Julia's type system is *parametric*, meaning that types can have parameters.

Type parameters are introduced after the name of the type, surrounded by curly braces:

```
struct Point{T<:Real}
    x::T
    y::T
end
```

This defines a new parametric type, `Point{T<:Real}`, holding two "coordinates" of type T, which can be any type having `Real` as supertype:

```
julia> Point(0.0, 0.0)
Point{Float64}(0.0, 0.0)
```

In addition to composite types, abstract types and primitive types can also have a type parameter.

> Having concrete types for struct fields is absolutely recommended for performance reasons, so this is a good way to make `Point` both fast and flexible.

Type Unions

A *type union* is an abstract parametric type that can act as any of its argument types:

```
julia> IntOrString = Union{Int64, String}
Union{Int64, String}
julia> 150 :: IntOrString
150
julia> "Julia" :: IntOrString
"Julia"
```

A type union in most computer languages is an internal construct for reasoning about types. Julia, however, exposes this feature to its users because efficient code can be generated when the type union has a small number of types. This feature gives the Julia programmer tremendous flexibility for controlling dispatch.

Methods

Methods can also be parametric, and objects can behave as functions.

Parametric Methods

Method definitions can also have type parameters qualifying their signature:

```
julia> isintpoint(p::Point{T}) where {T} = (T === Int64)
isintpoint (generic function with 1 method)
julia> p = Point(1, 2)
Point{Int64}(1, 2)
julia> isintpoint(p)
true
```

Function-like Objects

Any arbitrary Julia object can be made "callable." Such callable objects are sometimes called *functors*. For example:

```
struct Polynomial{R}
    coeff::Vector{R}
end

function (p::Polynomial)(x)
    val = p.coeff[end]
    for coeff in p.coeff[end-1:-1:1]
        val = val * x + coeff
    end
    val
end
```

To evaluate the polynomial, we simply have to call it:

```
julia> p = Polynomial([1,10,100])
Polynomial{Int64}([1, 10, 100])
julia> p(3)
931
```

Constructors

Parametric types can be explicitly or implicitly constructed:

```
julia> Point(1,2)        # implicit T
Point{Int64}(1, 2)
julia> Point{Int64}(1, 2) # explicit T
Point{Int64}(1, 2)
julia> Point(1,2.5)      # implicit T
ERROR: MethodError: no method matching Point(::Int64, ::Float64)
```

Default inner and outer constructors are generated for each T:

```
struct Point{T<:Real}
    x::T
    y::T
    Point{T}(x,y) where {T<:Real} = new(x,y)
end

Point(x::T, y::T) where {T<:Real} = Point{T}(x,y);
```

and both x and y have to be of the same type.

When x and y have a different type, the following outer constructor can be defined:

```
Point(x::Real, y::Real) = Point(promote(x,y)...);
```

The promote function is detailed in "Promotion" on page 231.

Conversion and Promotion

Julia has a system for promoting arguments to a common type. This is not done automatically but can be easily extended.

Conversion

A value can be *converted* from one type to another:

```
julia> x = 12
12
julia> typeof(x)
Int64
julia> convert(UInt8, x)
0x0c
julia> typeof(ans)
UInt8
```

We can also add our own convert methods:

```
julia> Base.convert(::Type{Point{T}}, x::Array{T, 1}) where {T<:Real} =
Point(x...)

julia> convert(Point{Int64}, [1, 2])
Point{Int64}(1, 2)
```

Promotion

Promotion is the conversion of values of mixed types to a single common type:

```
julia> promote(1, 2.5, 3)
(1.0, 2.5, 3.0)
```

Methods for the promote function are normally not directly defined, but the auxiliary function promote_rule is used to specify the rules for promotion:

```
promote_rule(::Type{Float64}, ::Type{Int32}) = Float64
```

Metaprogramming

Julia code can be represented as a data structure of the language itself. This allows a program to transform and generate its own code.

Expressions

Every Julia program starts as a string:

```
julia> prog = "1 + 2"
"1 + 2"
```

The next step is to parse each string into an object called an *expression*, represented by the Julia type Expr:

```
julia> ex = Meta.parse(prog)
:(1 + 2)
julia> typeof(ex)
Expr
julia> dump(ex)
Expr
  head: Symbol call
  args: Array{Any}((3,))
    1: Symbol +
    2: Int64 1
    3: Int64 2
```

The dump function displays expression objects with annotations.

Expressions can be constructed directly by prefixing with : inside parentheses or using a quote block:

```
julia> ex = quote
           1 + 2
       end;
```

eval

Julia can evaluate an expression object using eval:

```
julia> eval(ex)
3
```

Every module has its own eval function that evaluates expressions in its scope.

 When you are using a lot of calls to the function eval, often this means that something is wrong. eval is considered "evil."

Macros

Macros can include generated code in a program. A *macro* maps a tuple of `Expr` objects directly to a compiled expression.

Here is a simple macro:

```
macro containervariable(container, element)
    return esc(:($(Symbol(container,element)) = $container[$element]))
end
```

Macros are called by prefixing their name with the at sign (@). The macro call `@containervariable letters 1` is replaced by:

```
:(letters1 = letters[1])
```

`@macroexpand @containervariable letters 1` returns this expression, which is extremely useful for debugging.

This example illustrates how a macro can access the name of its arguments, something a function can't do. The return expression needs to be "escaped" with `esc` because it has to be resolved in the macro call environment.

Why use macros?

Macros generate and include fragments of customized code during parse time, thus *before* the full program is run.

Generated Functions

The macro `@generated` creates specialized code for methods depending on the types of the arguments:

```
@generated function square(x)
    println(x)
    :(x * x)
end
```

The body returns a quoted expression like a macro.

For the caller, the *generated function* behaves as a regular function:

```
julia> x = square(2); # note: output is from println() statement in the body
Int64
julia> x                # now we print x
4
julia> y = square("spam");
String
julia> y
"spamspam"
```

Missing Values

Missing values can be represented via the `missing` object, which is the singleton instance of the type `Missing`.

Arrays can contain missing values:

```
julia> a = [1, missing]
2-element Array{Union{Missing, Int64},1}:
 1
  missing
```

The element type of such an array is `Union{Missing, T}`, with `T` being the type of the non-missing values.

Reduction functions return `missing` when called on arrays that contain missing values:

```
julia> sum(a)
missing
```

In this situation, use the `skipmissing` function to skip missing values:

```
julia> sum(skipmissing([1, missing]))
1
```

Calling C and Fortran Code

A lot of code is written in C or Fortran. Reusing tested code is often better than writing your own version of an algorithm. Julia can call directly existing C or Fortran libraries using the `ccall` syntax.

In "Databases" on page 171 I introduced a Julia interface to the GDBM library of database functions. The library is written in C. To close the database a function call to `close(db)` has to be made:

```
Base.close(dbm::DBM) = gdbm_close(dbm.handle)

function gdbm_close(handle::Ptr{Cvoid})
    ccall((:gdbm_close, "libgdbm"), Cvoid, (Ptr{Cvoid},), handle)
end
```

A dbm object has a field `handle` of `Ptr{Cvoid}` type. This field holds a C pointer that refers to the database. To close the database the C function `gdbm_close` has to be called, having as its only argument the C pointer pointing to the database and no return value. Julia does this directly with the `ccall` function having as arguments:

- A tuple consisting of a symbol holding the name of the function we want to call, `:gdbm_close`, and the shared library specified as a string, `"libgdm"`

- The return type, `Cvoid`
- A tuple of argument types, `(Ptr{Cvoid},)`
- The argument values, `handle`

The complete mapping of the GDBM library can be found as an example in the ThinkJulia sources.

Glossary

named tuple
   A tuple with named components.

anonymous function
   A function defined without being given a name.

keyword arguments
   Arguments identified by name instead of only by position.

closure
   A function that captures variables from its defining scope.

block
   A way to group a number of statements.

let block
   A block allocating new variable bindings.

do block
   A syntax construction used to define and call an anonymous function that looks like a normal code block.

ternary operator
   A control flow operator taking three operands to specify a condition, an expression to be executed when the condition yields `true`, and an expression to be executed when the condition yields `false`.

short-circuit evaluation
   Evaluation of a Boolean operator where the second argument is executed or evaluated only if the first argument does not suffice to determine the value of the expression.

task (aka coroutine)
   A control flow feature that allows computations to be suspended and resumed in a flexible manner.

primitive type
> A concrete type whose data consists of plain old bits.

parametric type
> A type that is parameterized.

type union
> A type that includes as objects all instances of any of its type parameters.

functor
> An object that has an associated method, so that it is callable.

conversion
> Changing a value from one type to another.

promotion
> Converting values of mixed types to a single common type.

expression
> A Julia type that holds a language construct.

macro
> A way to include generated code in the final body of a program.

generated functions
> Functions capable of generating specialized code depending on the types of the arguments.

missing values
> Instances that represent data points with no value.

CHAPTER 20

The Goodies: Base and Standard Library

Julia comes with batteries included. The `Base` module contains the most useful functions, types, and macros. These are directly available in Julia.

Julia also provides a large number of specialized modules in its standard library for dates, distributed computing, linear algebra, profiling, random numbers, and more. Functions, types, and macros defined in the standard library have to be imported before they can be used:

- `import` *Module* imports the module, and *Module.fn*(x) calls the function *fn*.
- `using` *Module* imports all exported *Module* functions, types, and macros.

Additional functionality can be added from a growing collection of packages (*https://juliaobserver.com*).

This chapter is not intended as a replacement of the official Julia documentation (*https://docs.julialang.org*). The aim is merely to give some examples to illustrate what is possible, without being exhaustive. Functions already introduced elsewhere are not included.

Measuring Performance

We have seen that some algorithms perform better than others. The `fibonnaci` implementation from "Memos" on page 133 is a lot faster than the `fib` implementation from "One More Example" on page 71. The `@time` macro allows us to quantify the difference:

```
julia> fib(1)
1
julia> fibonacci(1)
```

```
      1
julia> @time fib(40)
  0.567546 seconds (5 allocations: 176 bytes)
102334155
julia> @time fibonacci(40)
  0.000012 seconds (8 allocations: 1.547 KiB)
102334155
```

@time prints the time the function took to execute, the number of allocations, and the allocated memory before returning the result. The memoized version is a lot faster but needs more memory.

There ain't no such thing as a free lunch!

A function in Julia is compiled the first time it is executed. So, to compare two algorithms, they have to be implemented as functions to get compiled and the first time they are called has to be excluded from the performance measure; otherwise, the compilation time is measured as well.

The package BenchmarkTools (*http://bit.ly/2K8hTwQ*) provides the macro @btime that does benchmarking the right way. Use it!

Collections and Data Structures

In "Dictionary Subtraction" on page 158 we used dictionaries to find the words that appear in a document but not in a word array. The function we wrote takes d1, which contains the words from the document as keys, and d2, which contains the array of words. It returns a dictionary that contains the keys from d1 that are not in d2:

```
function subtract(d1, d2)
    res = Dict()
    for key in keys(d1)
        if key ∉ keys(d2)
            res[key] = nothing
        end
    end
    res
end
```

In all of these dictionaries, the values are nothing because we never use them. As a result, we waste some storage space.

Julia provides another built-in type, called a *set*, that behaves like a collection of dictionary keys with no values. Adding elements to a set is fast; so is checking membership. And sets provide functions and operators to compute common set operations.

For example, set subtraction is available as a function called setdiff. So we can rewrite subtract like this:

```
function subtract(d1, d2)
    setdiff(d1, d2)
end
```

The result is a set instead of a dictionary.

Some of the exercises in this book can be done concisely and efficiently with sets. For example, here is a solution to "Exercise 10-7" on page 125 that uses a dictionary:

```
function hasduplicates(t)
    d = Dict()
    for x in t
        if x ∈ d
            return true
        end
        d[x] = nothing
    end
    false
end
```

When an element appears for the first time, it is added to the dictionary. If the same element appears again, the function returns true.

Using sets, we can write the same function like this:

```
function hasduplicates(t)
    length(Set(t)) < length(t)
end
```

An element can only appear in a set once, so if an element in t appears more than once, the set will be smaller than t. If there are no duplicates, the set will be the same size as t.

We can also use sets to do some of the exercises in Chapter 9. For example, here's a version of usesonly with a loop:

```
function usesonly(word, available)
    for letter in word
        if letter ∉ available
            return false
        end
    end
    true
end
```

usesonly checks whether all the letters in word are in available. We can rewrite it like this:

```
function usesonly(word, available)
    Set(word) ⊆ Set(available)
end
```

The ⊆ (**\subseteq** **TAB**) operator checks whether one set is a subset of another, including the possibility that they are equal, which is true if all the letters in `word` appear in `available`.

Exercise 20-1

Rewrite `avoids` using sets.

Mathematics

Complex numbers are also supported in Julia. The global constant `im` is bound to the complex number i, representing the principal square root of -1.

We can now verify Euler's identity:

```
julia> e^(im*π)+1
0.0 + 1.2246467991473532e-16im
```

The symbol e (**\euler** **TAB**) is the base of natural logarithms.

Let's illustrate the complex nature of trigonometric functions:

$$\cos(x) = \frac{e^{ix} + e^{-ix}}{2}$$

We can test this formula for different values of x:

```
julia> x = 0:0.1:2π
0.0:0.1:6.2
julia> cos.(x) == 0.5*(e.^(im*x)+e.^(-im*x))
true
```

Here, another example of the dot operator is shown. Julia also allows numeric literals to be juxtaposed with identifiers as coefficients, as in 2π.

Strings

In Chapters 8 and 9, we did some elementary searches in string objects. Julia can also handle Perl-compatible regular expressions (*regexes*), which eases the task of finding complex patterns in string objects.

The `usesonly` function can be implemented as a regex:

```
function usesonly(word, available)
  r = Regex("[^$(available)]")
  !occursin(r, word)
end
```

The regex looks for a character that is not in the available string and occursin returns true if the pattern is found in word:

```
julia> usesonly("banana", "abn")
true
julia> usesonly("bananas", "abn")
false
```

Regexes can also be constructed as nonstandard string literals prefixed with r:

```
julia> match(r"[^abn]", "banana")

julia> m = match(r"[^abn]", "bananas")
RegexMatch("s")
```

String interpolation is not allowed in this case. The match function returns nothing if the pattern (a command) is not found and a RegexMatch object otherwise.

We can extract the following information from a RegexMatch object:

- The entire substring matched (m.match)
- The captured substrings as an array of strings (m.captures)
- The offset at which the whole match begins (m.offset)
- The offsets of the captured substrings as an array (m.offsets)

For example:

```
julia> m.match
"s"
julia> m.offset
7
```

Regexes are extremely powerful and the perlre mainpage (*http://bit.ly/2VijnFY*) provides all the details to construct the most exotic searches.

Arrays

In Chapter 10 we used an array object as a one-dimensional container with an index to address its elements. In Julia, however, arrays are multidimensional collections, or *matrices*.

Let's create a 2-by-3 zero matrix:

```
julia> z = zeros(Float64, 2, 3)
2×3 Array{Float64,2}:
 0.0  0.0  0.0
 0.0  0.0  0.0
julia> typeof(z)
Array{Float64,2}
```

The type of this matrix is an array holding floating points and having two dimensions.

The size function returns a tuple with as elements the number of elements in each dimension:

```
julia> size(z)
(2, 3)
```

The function ones constructs a matrix with unit value elements:

```
julia> s = ones(String, 1, 3)
1×3 Array{String,2}:
 ""  ""  ""
```

The string unit element is an empty string.

 s is not a one-dimensional array:

```
julia> s == ["", "", ""]
false
```

s is a row matrix and ["", "", ""] is a column matrix.

A matrix can be entered directly using a space to separate elements in a row and a semicolon (;) to separate rows:

```
julia> a = [1 2 3; 4 5 6]
2×3 Array{Int64,2}:
 1  2  3
 4  5  6
```

You can use square brackets to address individual elements:

```
julia> z[1,2] = 1
1
julia> z[2,3] = 1
1
julia> z
2×3 Array{Float64,2}:
 0.0  1.0  0.0
 0.0  0.0  1.0
```

Slices can be used for each dimension to select a subgroup of elements:

```
julia> u = z[:,2:end]
2×2 Array{Float64,2}:
 1.0  0.0
 0.0  1.0
```

The . operator broadcasts to all dimensions:

```
julia> e.^(im*u)
2×2 Array{Complex{Float64},2}:
```

```
 0.540302+0.841471im       1.0+0.0im
      1.0+0.0im        0.540302+0.841471im
```

Interfaces

Julia specifies some informal interfaces to define behaviors—i.e., methods with a specific goal. When you extend such a method for a type, objects of that type can be used to build upon these behaviors.

If it looks like a duck, swims like a duck, and quacks like a duck, then it probably *is* a duck.

Looping over the values of a collection (iteration) is such an interface. In "One More Example" on page 71 we implemented the fib function, returning the *n*th element of the Fibonacci sequence. Let's make an iterator that lazily returns the Fibonacci sequence:

```
struct Fibonacci{T<:Real} end
Fibonacci(d::DataType) = d<:Real ? Fibonacci{d}() : error("No Real type!")

Base.iterate(::Fibonacci{T}) where {T<:Real} = (zero(T), (one(T), one(T)))
Base.iterate(::Fibonacci{T}, state::Tuple{T, T}) where {T<:Real} = (state[1],
(state[2], state[1] + state[2]))
```

Here, we implemented a parametric type with no fields (Fibonacci), an outer constructor, and two iterate methods. The first is called to initialize the iterator and returns a tuple consisting of the first value, 0, and a state. The state in this case is a tuple containing the second and third values, 1 and 1.

The second method is called to get the next value of the Fibonacci sequence. It returns a tuple having as its first element the next value and as its second element the state, which is a tuple with the two following values.

We can use Fibonacci now in a for loop:

```
julia> for e in Fibonacci(Int64)
           e > 100 && break
           print(e, " ")
       end
0 1 1 2 3 5 8 13 21 34 55 89
```

It looks like magic has happened, but the explanation is simple. A for loop in Julia:

```
for i in iter
    # body
end
```

is translated into:

```
next = iterate(iter)
while next !== nothing
    (i, state) = next
    # body
    next = iterate(iter, state)
end
```

This is a great example of how a well-defined interface allows an implementation to use all the functions that are aware of the interface.

Interactive Utilities

We already met the `InteractiveUtils` module, in "Debugging" on page 217. But the `@which` macro is only the tip of the iceberg.

The LLVM library transforms Julia code into *machine code*—instructions that the computer's CPU can execute directly—in multiple steps. We can directly visualize the output of each stage.

Let's take a look at a simple example:

```
function squaresum(a::Float64, b::Float64)
    a^2 + b^2
end
```

The first step is to look at the "lowered" code:

```
julia> using InteractiveUtils

julia> @code_lowered squaresum(3.0, 4.0)
CodeInfo(
1 ─ %1 = (Core.apply_type)(Base.Val, 2)
│   %2 = (%1)()
│   %3 = (Base.literal_pow)(:^, a, %2)
│   %4 = (Core.apply_type)(Base.Val, 2)
│   %5 = (%4)()
│   %6 = (Base.literal_pow)(:^, b, %5)
│   %7 = %3 + %6
└──      return %7
)
```

The `@code_lowered` macro returns an array of an *intermediate representation* of the code that is used by the compiler to generate optimized code.

The next step adds type information:

```
julia> @code_typed squaresum(3.0, 4.0)
CodeInfo(
1 ─ %1 = (Base.mul_float)(a, a)::Float64
│   %2 = (Base.mul_float)(b, b)::Float64
```

```
|    %3 = (Base.add_float)(%1, %2)::Float64
└──      return %3
) => Float64
```

We see that the type of the intermediate results and the return value are correctly inferred.

This representation of the code is now transformed into LLVM code:

```
julia> @code_llvm squaresum(3.0, 4.0)
;  @ none:2 within `squaresum'
define double @julia_squaresum_14823(double, double) {
top:
; ┌ @ intfuncs.jl:243 within `literal_pow'
; │┌ @ float.jl:399 within `*'
    %2 = fmul double %0, %0
    %3 = fmul double %1, %1
; └└
; ┌ @ float.jl:395 within `+'
   %4 = fadd double %2, %3
; └
   ret double %4
}
```

And finally the machine code is generated:

```
julia> @code_native squaresum(3.0, 4.0)
        .section        __TEXT,__text,regular,pure_instructions
; ┌ @ none:2 within `squaresum'
; │┌ @ intfuncs.jl:243 within `literal_pow'
; ││┌ @ none:2 within `*'
        vmulsd  %xmm0, %xmm0, %xmm0
        vmulsd  %xmm1, %xmm1, %xmm1
; │└└
; │┌ @ float.jl:395 within `+'
        vaddsd  %xmm1, %xmm0, %xmm0
; │└
        retl
        nopl    (%eax)
; └
```

Debugging

The Logging macros provide an alternative to scaffolding with print statements:

```
julia> @warn "Abandon printf debugging, all ye who enter here!"
┌ Warning: Abandon printf debugging, all ye who enter here!
└ @ Main REPL[1]:1
```

The debug statements don't have to be removed from the source. For example, in contrast to the @warn above, this will produce no output by default:

```
julia> @debug "The sum of some values $(sum(rand(100)))"
```

In this case, sum(rand(100)) will never be evaluated unless *debug logging* is enabled to store the debug messages in a log file.

The level of logging can be selected by an environment variable, JULIA_DEBUG:

```
$ JULIA_DEBUG=all julia -e '@debug "The sum of some values $(sum(rand(100)))"'
┌ Debug: The sum of some values 47.116520814555024
└ @ Main none:1
```

Here, we have used all to get all debug information, but you can also choose to generate only output for a specific file or module.

Glossary

set
> A collection of distinct objects.

regex
> A regular expression, or sequence of characters that define a search pattern.

matrix
> A two-dimensional array.

machine code
> Language instructions that can be executed directly by a computer's central processing unit.

intermediate representation
> A data structure used internally by a compiler to represent source code.

debug logging
> Storing debug messages in a log.

CHAPTER 21

Debugging

When you are debugging, you should distinguish among different kinds of errors in order to track them down more quickly:

- *Syntax errors* are discovered by the interpreter when it is translating the source code into byte code. They indicate that there is something wrong with the structure of the program. Example: Omitting the end keyword at the end of a function block generates the somewhat redundant message ERROR: LoadError: syntax: incomplete: function requires end.

- *Runtime errors* are produced by the interpreter if something goes wrong while the program is running. Most runtime error messages include information about where the error occurred and what functions were executing. Example: An infinite recursion eventually causes the runtime error ERROR: StackOverflowError.

- *Semantic errors* are problems with a program that runs without producing error messages but doesn't do the right thing. Example: An expression may not be evaluated in the order you expect, yielding an incorrect result.

The first step in debugging is to figure out which kind of error you are dealing with. Although the following sections are organized by error type, some techniques are applicable in more than one situation.

Syntax Errors

Syntax errors are usually easy to fix once you figure out what they are. Unfortunately, the error messages are often not helpful. The most common messages are ERROR: LoadError: syntax: incomplete: premature end of input and ERROR: LoadError: syntax: unexpected "=", neither of which is very informative.

On the other hand, the message does tell you where in the program the problem occurred. Actually, it tells you where Julia noticed a problem, which is not necessarily where the error is. Sometimes the error is prior to the location of the error message, often on the preceding line.

If you are building the program incrementally, you should have a good idea about where the error is. It will be in the last line you added.

If you are copying code from a book, start by comparing your code to the book's code very carefully. Check every character. At the same time, remember that the book might be wrong, so if you see something that looks like a syntax error, it might be.

Here are some ways to avoid the most common syntax errors:

1. Make sure you are not using a Julia keyword for a variable name.

2. Check that you have the end keyword at the end of every compound statement, including for, while, if, and function blocks.

3. Make sure that any strings in the code have matching quotation marks. Make sure that all quotation marks are "straight quotes," not "curly quotes."

4. If you have multiline strings with triple quotes, make sure you have terminated the strings properly. An unterminated string may cause an invalid token error at the end of your program, or the compiler may treat the following part of the program as a string until it comes to the next string. In the second case, it might not produce an error message at all!

5. An unclosed opening operator—(, {, or [—makes Julia continue with the next line as part of the current statement. Generally, an error occurs almost immediately in the next line.

6. Check for the classic = instead of == inside a conditional.

7. If you have nonASCII characters in the code (including strings and comments), that might cause a problem, although Julia usually handles nonASCII characters. Be careful if you paste in text from a web page or other source.

If none of these suggestions work, move on to the next section....

I Keep Making Changes and It Makes No Difference

If the REPL says there is an error and you don't see it, that might be because you and the REPL are not looking at the same code. Check your programming environment to make sure that the program you are editing is the one Julia is trying to run.

If you are not sure, try putting an obvious and deliberate syntax error at the beginning of the program. Now run it again. If the REPL doesn't find the new error, you are not running the new code.

There are a few likely culprits:

- You edited the file and forgot to save the changes before running it again. Some programming environments do this for you, but some don't.
- You changed the name of the file, but you are still running the old name.
- Something in your development environment is configured incorrectly.
- If you are writing a module and using using, make sure you don't give your module the same name as one of the standard Julia modules.
- If you are using using to import a module, remember that you have to restart the REPL when you modify the code in the module. If you import the module again, it doesn't do anything.

If you get stuck and you can't figure out what is going on, one approach is to start again with a new program like "Hello, World!" and make sure you can get the known program to run. Then gradually add the pieces of the original program to the new one.

Runtime Errors

Once your program is syntactically correct, Julia can read it and at least start running it. What could possibly go wrong?

My Program Does Absolutely Nothing

This problem is most common when your file consists of functions and classes but does not actually invoke a function to start execution. This may be intentional if you only plan to import this module to supply classes and functions.

If it is not intentional, make sure there is a function call in the program, and make sure the flow of execution reaches it (see "Flow of execution" on page 251).

My Program Hangs

If a program stops and seems to be doing nothing, it is "hanging." Often that means that it is caught in an infinite loop or infinite recursion. Here are a few tips that can help you identify the problem:

- If there is a particular loop that you suspect is the problem, add a print statement immediately before the loop that says "entering the loop" and another immediately after that says "exiting the loop."

  Run the program. If you get the first message and not the second, you've got an infinite loop. Go to "Infinite loop" on page 250.

- Most of the time, an infinite recursion will cause the program to run for a while and then produce an `ERROR: LoadError: StackOverflowError` error. If that happens, go to "Infinite recursion" on page 250.

  If you are not getting this error but you suspect there is a problem with a recursive method or function, you can still use the techniques described in that section.

- If neither of those steps works, start testing other loops and other recursive functions and methods.

- If that doesn't work, then it is possible that you don't understand the flow of execution in your program. Go to "Flow of execution" on page 251.

Infinite loop

When you think you've identified an infinite loop, add a print statement at the end of the loop that prints the values of the variables in the condition and the value of the condition.

For example:

```
while x > 0 && y < 0
    # do something to x
    # do something to y
    @debug "variables" x y
    @debug "condition" x > 0 && y < 0
end
```

Now when you run the program in debug mode, you will see the values of the variables and the condition for each time through the loop. The last time through the loop, the condition should be `false`. If the loop keeps going, you will be able to see the values of x and y, and you might be able to figure out why they are not being updated correctly.

Infinite recursion

If you suspect that a function is causing an infinite recursion, make sure that there is a base case. There should be some condition that causes the function to return without making a recursive invocation. If not, you need to rethink the algorithm and identify a base case.

If there is a base case but the program doesn't seem to be reaching it, add a print statement at the beginning of the function that prints the parameters. Now when you run the program, you will see a few lines of output every time the function is invoked, and you will see the parameter values. If the parameters are not moving toward the base case, you will get some ideas about why not.

Flow of execution

If you are not sure how the flow of execution is moving through your program, add print statements to the beginning of each function with a message like "entering function *foo*", where *foo* is the name of the function.

Now when you run the program, it will print a trace of each function as it is invoked.

When I Run the Program I Get an Exception

If something goes wrong during runtime, Julia prints a message that includes the name of the exception, the line of the program where the problem occurred, and a stacktrace.

The stacktrace identifies the function that is currently running, and then the function that called it, and then the function that called that, and so on. In other words, it traces the sequence of function calls that got you to where you are, including the line number in your file where each call occurred.

The first step is to examine the place in the program where the error occurred and see if you can figure out what happened. These are some of the most common runtime errors:

ArgumentError
: One of the arguments to a function call is not in the expected state.

BoundsError
: An indexing operation into an array tried to access an out-of-bounds element.

DivideError
: Integer division was attempted with a denominator value of 0.

DomainError
: The argument to a function or constructor is outside the valid domain.

EOFError
: No more data is available to read from a file or stream.

InexactError
: The value cannot be converted exactly to a type.

KeyError
: An indexing operation into an AbstractDict (Dict)- or Set-like object tried to access or delete a nonexistent element.

MethodError
: A method with the required type signature does not exist in the given generic function. Alternatively, there is no unique most specific method.

OutOfMemoryError
: An operation allocated too much memory for either the system or the garbage collector to handle properly.

OverflowError
: The result of an expression is too large for the specified type and will cause a wraparound.

StackOverflowError
: The function call grew beyond the size of the call stack. This usually happens when a call recurses infinitely.

StringIndexError
: An error occurred when trying to access a string at an index that is not valid.

SystemError
: A system call failed with an error code.

TypeError
: A type assertion failure has occurred, or you've called an intrinsic function with an incorrect argument type.

UndefVarError
: A symbol in the current scope is not defined.

I Added So Many print Statements I Get Inundated with Output

One of the problems with using print statements for debugging is that you can end up buried in output. There are two ways to proceed: simplify the output or simplify the program.

To simplify the output, you can remove or comment out print statements that aren't helping, or combine them, or format the output so it is easier to understand.

To simplify the program, there are several things you can do. First, scale down the problem the program is working on. For example, if you are searching a list, search a small list. If the program takes input from the user, give it the simplest input that causes the problem.

Second, clean up the program. Remove dead code and reorganize the program to make it as easy to read as possible. For example, if you suspect that the problem is in a deeply nested part of the program, try rewriting that part with a simpler structure. If you suspect a large function, try splitting it into smaller functions and testing them separately.

Often the process of finding the minimal test case leads you to the bug. If you find that a program works in one situation but not in another, that gives you a clue about what is going on.

Similarly, rewriting a piece of code can help you find subtle bugs. If you make a change that you think shouldn't affect the program, and it does, that can tip you off.

Semantic Errors

In some ways, semantic errors are the hardest to debug, because the interpreter provides no information about what is wrong. Only you know what the program is supposed to do.

The first step is to make a connection between the program text and the behavior you are seeing. You need a hypothesis about what the program is actually doing. One of the things that makes that hard is that computers run so fast.

You will often wish that you could slow the program down to human speed. Inserting a few well-placed print statements is often quicker than setting up a debugger, inserting and removing breakpoints, and "stepping" the program to where the error is occurring.

My Program Doesn't Work

Ask yourself these questions:

- Is there something the program was supposed to do but that doesn't seem to be happening? Find the section of the code that performs that function and make sure it is executing when you think it should.

- Is something happening that shouldn't? Find code in your program that performs that function and see if it is executing when it shouldn't.

- Is a section of code producing an effect that is not what you expected? Make sure that you understand the code in question, especially if it involves functions or methods in other Julia modules. Read the documentation for the functions you call. Try them out by writing simple test cases and checking the results.

In order to program, you need a mental model of how programs work. If you write a program that doesn't do what you expect, often the problem is not in the program; it's in your mental model.

The best way to correct your mental model is to break the program into its components (usually the functions and methods) and test each component independently. Once you find the discrepancy between your model and reality, you can solve the problem.

Of course, you should be building and testing components as you develop the program. If you encounter a problem, there should be only a small amount of new code that is not known to be correct.

I've Got a Big Hairy Expression and It Doesn't Do What I Expect

Writing complex expressions is fine as long as they are readable, but they can be hard to debug. It is often a good idea to break a complex expression into a series of assignments to temporary variables.

For example, this:

```
addcard(game.hands[i], popcard(game.hands[findneighbor(game, i)]))
```

can be rewritten as:

```
neighbor = findneighbor(game, i)
pickedcard = popcard(game.hands[neighbor])
addcard(game.hands[i], pickedcard)
```

The explicit version is easier to read because the variable names provide additional documentation, and it is easier to debug because you can check the types of the intermediate variables and display their values.

Another problem that can occur with big expressions is that the order of evaluation may not be what you expect. For example, if you are translating the expression $\frac{x}{2\pi}$ into Julia, you might write:

```
y = x / 2 * π
```

That is not correct because multiplication and division have the same precedence and are evaluated from left to right. So this expression computes $\frac{x\pi}{2}$.

A good way to debug expressions is to add parentheses to make the order of evaluation explicit:

```
y = x / (2 * π)
```

Whenever you are not sure of the order of evaluation, use parentheses. Not only will the program be correct (in the sense of doing what you intended), it will also be more readable for other people who haven't memorized the order of operations.

I've Got a Function That Doesn't Return What I Expect

If you have a `return` statement with a complex expression, you don't have a chance to print the result before returning. Again, you can use a temporary variable. For example, instead of:

```
return removematches(game.hands[i])
```

you could write:

```
count = removematches(game.hands[i])
return count
```

Now you have the opportunity to display the value of count before returning.

I'm Really, Really Stuck and I Need Help

First, try getting away from the computer for a few minutes. Working with a computer can cause these symptoms:

- Frustration and rage
- Superstitious beliefs ("the computer hates me") and magical thinking ("the program only works when I wear my hat backward") *
- Random walk programming (the attempt to program by writing every possible program and choosing the one that does the right thing)

If you find yourself suffering from any of these symptoms, get up and go for a walk. When you are calm, think about the program. What is it doing? What are some possible causes of that behavior? When was the last time you had a working program, and what did you do next?

Sometimes it just takes time to find a bug. I often find bugs when I am away from the computer and let my mind wander. Some of the best places to find bugs are on trains, in the shower, and in bed, just before you fall asleep. ø

No, I Really Need Help

It happens. Even the best programmers occasionally get stuck. Sometimes you work on a program so long that you can't see the error. You need a fresh pair of eyes.

Before you bring someone else in, make sure you are prepared. Your program should be as simple as possible, and you should be working on the smallest input that causes the error. You should have print statements in the appropriate places (and the output they produce should be comprehensible). You should understand the problem well enough to describe it concisely.

When you bring someone in to help, be sure to give them the information they need:

- If there is an error message, what is it and what part of the program does it indicate?
- What was the last thing you did before this error occurred? What were the last lines of code that you wrote, or what is the new test case that fails?
- What have you tried so far, and what have you learned?

When you find the bug, take a second to think about what you could have done to find it faster. Next time you see something similar, you will be able to find the bug more quickly.

Remember, the goal is not just to make the program work. The goal is to learn how to make the program work.

Unicode Input

The following table lists a few Unicode characters out of many that can be entered via tab completion of LaTeX-like abbreviations in the Julia REPL (and in various other editing environments).

Character	Tab completion sequence	ASCII representation
²	\^2	
₁	_1	
₂	_2	
🍎	\:apple:	
🍌	\:banana:	
🐫	\:camel:	
🍐	\:pear:	
🐢	\:turtle:	
∩	\cap	
≡	\equiv	===
ℯ	\euler	
∈	\in	in
≥	\ge	>=
≤	\le	<=
≠	\ne	!=
∉	\notin	
π	\pi	pi
⊆	\subseteq	
ε	\varepsilon	

JuliaBox

JuliaBox allows you to run Julia in your browser. Enter the URL *https://www.julia box.com*, log in, and start using the Jupyter environment.

The initial screen is shown in Figure B-1. The new button allows the creation of a Julia notebook, a text file, a folder, or a terminal session.

In a terminal session, the command `julia` starts the REPL as shown in Figure B-2.

The notebook interface allows you to mix text in Markdown markup and highlighted code with associated output. Figure B-3 shows an example.

Further documentation can be found on the Jupyter website (*http://jupyter.org/docu mentation*).

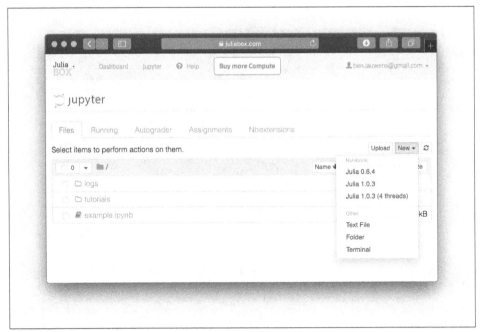

Figure B-1. Initial screen

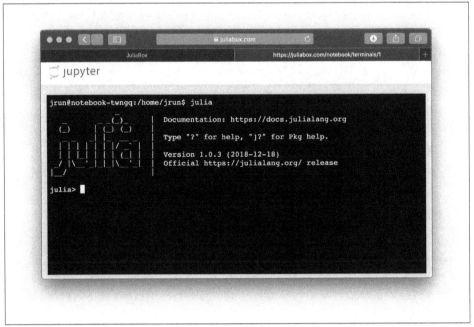

Figure B-2. Terminal session

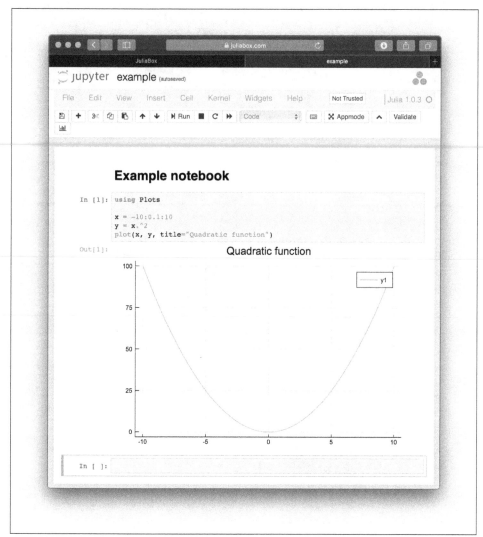

Figure B-3. Notebook

Index

Symbols

+ (addition operator), 3, 15
&& (and operator), 51, 227
-> (arrow), in anonymous function, 224
=> (arrow), in key-value pair, 128
* (asterisk)
    concatenation operator, 15
    multiplication operator, 3, 15
@ (at sign), preceding macros, 233
`...` (backticks), enclosing commands, 173
[...] (bracket operator)
    enclosing array elements, 109
    enclosing array indices, 110
    enclosing array slices, 112, 120
    enclosing dictionary keys, 127, 128
    enclosing matrix elements, 242
    enclosing string indices, 88
    enclosing string slices, 90
    enclosing tuple indices, 142
^ (caret)
    concatenation repetition operator, 15
    exponentiation operator, 4, 15
: (colon)
    for array slice, 112, 120
    preceding constructed expressions, 232
    preceding object field names, 185
    for string slice, 90
, (comma)
    not using in integers, 4
    separating tuple elements, 141
{...} (curly braces)
    enclosing dictionary types, 127
    enclosing parametric types, 229
/ (division operator), 4, 15

$ (dollar sign), for string interpolation, 91
. (dot syntax)
    with functions, 115, 123
    with named tuples, 223
    with object fields, 180, 181
    with operators, 115, 123, 242
… (ellipsis), following parameter name, 144
= (equal sign)
    assignment operator, 11, 77
    specifying default values, 157, 200
== (equal to operator), 50, 184
=== (equivalent to operator), 117, 184
$\equiv$ (equivalent to operator), 117, 184
! (exclamation point), in function names, 113, 191
! (factorial symbol), 69
$\div$ (floor division operator), 49, 58
> (greater than operator), 50
>= (greater than or equal to operator), 50
$\geq$ (greater than or equal to operator), 50
$\in$ (in operator), 94, 111, 128
< (less than operator), 50
<= (less than or equal to operator), 50
$\leq$ (less than or equal to operator), 50
% (modulus operator), 49, 58
! (not operator), 51
!= (not equal to operator), 50
$\neq$ (not equal to operator), 50
$\notin$ (not in operator), 103
(number sign), preceding comments, 16
|| (or operator), 51, 227
(...) (parentheses)
    enclosing tuple elements, 141
    in expressions, 14, 254

division
    division operator (/), 4, 15
    divrem function, 143
    remainder from, 49, 143
do blocks, 226, 235
docstring, 43, 45
    (see also comments)
dollar sign ($), for string interpolation, 91
DomainError, 251
dot operators, 115, 123, 242
dot syntax (.)
    with functions, 115, 123
    with named tuples, 223
    with object fields, 180, 181
    with operators, 115, 123, 242
dump function, 175, 232

E

eachindex function, 111
eachline function, 102
echo command, 174
ellipsis (…), following parameter name, 144
else keyword, 51
elseif keyword, 52
embedded objects, 182, 186
empty array, 109, 112
empty string, 91, 97
empty tuple, 142
encapsulation
    of code, in functions, 39, 44
    of data, 218, 220
encapsulation and generalization process, 42
encode, 209, 219
end keyword, 51, 225, 248
    in arrays, 111
    in for statement, 37
    in functions, 23
    in strings, 91
enumerate function, 146
EOFError, 251
equal sign (=)
    assignment operator, 11, 77
    specifying default values, 157, 200
equal to operator (==), 50, 184
equality
    compared to assignment, 50, 77
    for floating-point values, 83
    operators for (see relational operators)
equivalent objects, 118, 123

equivalent to operator (===), 117, 184
equivalent to operator (≡), 117, 184
error function, 132
errors (bugs), 6, 8
    (see also debugging)
    ArgumentError, 21, 57, 251
    BoundsError, 96, 143, 251
    DivideError, 251
    DomainError, 251
    EOFError, 251
    InexactError, 251
    KeyError, 128, 251
    list of, 251
    LoadError, 247
    MethodError, 88, 91, 142, 144, 199, 230, 251
    OutOfMemoryError, 252
    OverflowError, 252
    runtime errors, 17, 57, 247, 249-253
    semantic errors, 17, 247, 253-256
    shape error, 149, 150
    StackOverflowError, 56, 72, 247, 250, 252
    stacktrace for, 28, 32, 56, 251
    StringIndexError, 252
    syntax errors, 16, 57, 247-249
    SystemError, 170, 252
    TypeError, 197, 252
    types of, 16, 247
    UndefVarError, 27, 78, 136, 226, 252
eval function, 232
evaluation of expressions, 13, 17, 232
    (see also operators, precedence of)
exceptions, 17, 18
    (see also runtime errors)
    catching, 170, 176
    generating, 132
exclamation point (!), in function names, 113, 191
execution
    flow of, 25, 31, 71, 249, 251
    in REPL, 13, 18
exponentiation operator (^), 4, 15
export statement, 174
Expr type, 232
expression objects, 232
expressions, 12, 17, 236
    boolean, 50, 58
    composition of, 23, 31, 67
    debugging, 254
    evaluation of, 13, 17, 232

About the Authors

Ben Lauwens is a professor of mathematics at the Royal Military Academy (RMA Belgium). He has a PhD in engineering and master's degrees from KU Leuven and RMA and a bachelor's degree from RMA.

Allen B. Downey is a professor of computer science at Olin College of Engineering. He has taught at Wellesley College, Colby College, and UC Berkeley. He has a PhD in computer science from UC Berkeley and master's and bachelor's degrees from MIT.

Colophon

The animal on the cover of *Think Julia* is the snowy owl (*Bubo scandiacus*), a bird of prey native to the Arctic tundra in North America and Eurasia. It winters in lower latitudes, and regularly can be seen in windswept fields or coastal dunes in the northern United States. Weighing in at about four pounds, it is North America's largest owl.

The snowy owl's distinctive yellow eyes and black beak make it easily recognizable. Female owls maintain barred dark brown feathers throughout their lives, while males lose this coloring as they mature, becoming pale white.

Unlike most owls, the snowy owl hunts during the day, by either swooping from a perch or flying low to the ground. It can eat more than 1,600 lemmings in a single year, and bases its nesting cycle on the current lemming population. While they seem to prefer lemmings, snowy owls also feed on a variety of rodents, as well as the occasional fish or fellow bird.

Many readers will be familiar with Hedwig, probably the most famous (albeit fictional) snowy owl in the 21st century, who serves as Harry's dignified pet and courier in the *Harry Potter* series.

The snowy owl's current conservation status was escalated to Vulnerable in 2017, with an estimated wild population of 28,000 individuals at the time. Many of the animals on O'Reilly covers are endangered; all of them are important to the world.

The cover illustration is by Karen Montgomery, based on a black and white engraving from *British Birds*. The cover fonts are Gilroy Semibold and Guardian Sans. The text font is Adobe Minion Pro; the heading font is Adobe Myriad Condensed; and the code font is Dalton Maag's Ubuntu Mono.

O'REILLY®

There's much more
where this came from.

Experience books, videos, live online
training courses, and more from O'Reilly
and our 200+ partners—all in one place.

Learn more at oreilly.com/online-learning

CPSIA information can be obtained
at www.ICGtesting.com
Printed in the USA
LVHW011606030722
722665LV00006B/248